LEADING
BEYOND
BOUNDARIES

DR. COREY HAMILTON

Unlocking the Power of
Culturally Diverse Leadership

Leading Beyond Boundaries: Unlocking the Power of Culturally Diverse Leadership

DR. COREY HAMILTON

Copyright © 2023 by Home Again Publishing

While the author has made every effort to provide up-to-date information at the time of publication, neither the publisher nor the author assumes any responsibility for errors, or for changes that occur after publication. Further, the publisher has no control over and does not assume any responsibility for author or third-party websites or their contents.

Printed in the United States of America

First Printing, 2023

BOOK DESIGN BY USEDTOTECH.COM

ISBN 979-8-9887015-7-6

Home Again Publishing
5606 SMU BLVD 601091
DALLAS, TX 75360

Dedication

Thank you to the one who sacrificed it all—the trailblazers, elders, and those who endured hardship to advance diversity, equity, and inclusion in the most difficult of places.

"Let us, therefore, make every effort to do what leads to peace and to mutual edification."

Romans 14:19

Table of Contents

EMBRACING DIVERSITY: A NOTE FROM THE AUTHOR

To You, Valued Reader:

As I take a moment to reflect on the journey that led to the creation of this book, my heart is filled with gratitude and excitement. Leading Beyond Boundaries has been a labor of love, inspired by a profound desire to inspire positive change and foster real, meaningful conversations about diversity, equity, and inclusion.

The changing landscape of our world calls for a new narrative—one that celebrates the strength of our differences and empowers every individual to embrace their authentic selves. Through these pages, I sought to provide stories and examples that highlight the transformative potential of minority leadership. Each chapter is an exploration into the power of identity, experience, and resilience in shaping the leaders of tomorrow.

This book is not just a collection of words; it is a call to action. It is an invitation to open our hearts and minds, to embrace the richness of diversity, and to dismantle the barriers that hinder progress. My hope is that you, dear reader, will find inspiration within these pages to drive positive change in your life and community.

In delving into the wisdom of experience, the importance of allies and advocates, and the resilience needed to overcome obstacles, I aimed to offer practical insights that go beyond theory and resonate with your personal journey. I want this book to serve as a guiding light, illuminating the path to a more inclusive and equitable world.

Your engagement with this work is a crucial part of the journey. This book is not designed to be a tool for symbolic gestures. It is meant to be used as a guide to inject real change. By reading these chapters, immersing yourself in this catalog of diversity knowledge, and transparently answering questions at the end of each chapter, you become an integral part of the action-oriented conversation. Your willingness to explore these themes with an open heart and mind is a testament to your commitment to positive change.

I extend my heartfelt appreciation to you for joining me on this quest for understanding and growth. The reader-author relationship is a powerful one, and I am honored to have you as a companion on this journey. Your presence in this shared space elevates the impact of these words, making them catalysts for transformation.

As you delve into each chapter, I encourage you to reflect on your own experiences and insights. Embrace the power of dialogue and engage in meaningful conversations with others. Let this book be the spark that ignites change in your own life and ripples outwards to create a lasting impact in the world.

Together, let us champion the cause of diversity, equity, and inclusion. Let us break down the barriers that hold us back and build supportive cultures that uplift every voice. Let us play the infinite game of minority leadership, where the goal is not merely to win but to create a world where every individual can thrive.

Thank you for being an integral part of this journey. Your commitment to reading, learning, and growing inspires me as an author, and it reaffirms the power of maximizing united communities to drive positive change. I look forward to connecting with you through these pages and beyond.

With deep gratitude and warm regards,

Dr. Corey L. Hamilton

(Author of Leading Beyond Boundaries)

In the realm of pages, rich with hues,

A tapestry of cultures, a story to peruse,

A book unfolds with History's grace,

Diving deep into diversity's embrace.

Oh, reader, come and take a seat,

In History's rhythm, let's meet and greet,

A tale of leaders bold and true,

In every shade, in every hue.

From Harlem's streets to distant lands,

The book unfurls in History's hands,

Leaders rise, their voices strong,

For cultural diversity, they sing the song.

So, turn the pages, let wisdom flow,

In History's echo, let's gently go,

Exploring lands both near and far,

Guided by his poetic star.

In the tapestry of cultures we weave,

History's legacy, in every leave,

Let this book inspire, uplift, and inspire,

In History's spirit, let's never tire.

Home Again Publishing

Leading Beyond Boundaries:

Unlocking the Power of Culturally Diverse Leadership

CHAPTER ONE

Unlocking the Power of Minority Leadership

"

Diversity in leadership encompasses the intersectionality of identities, including race, ethnicity, gender, age, sexual orientation, and disability, among others.

In today's rapidly changing and interconnected world, harnessing the power of minority leadership has become increasingly vital for organizations seeking to thrive and excel in diverse environments. As we navigate this chapter, we will delve into the transformative potential of minority leadership, exploring the unique perspectives, insights, and contributions that minority leaders bring to organizations. By recognizing the value of diverse leadership and understanding the challenges faced by minority leaders, we can unlock untapped potential and pave the way for inclusive and impactful leadership that drives organizational success.

Diversity in leadership encompasses the intersectionality of identities, including race, ethnicity, gender, age, sexual orientation, and disability. This diverse range of backgrounds and experiences brings forth a wealth of knowledge, fresh perspectives, and innovative ideas that propel organizations forward. By embracing diversity in leadership, organizations also embrace the collective strengths of their diverse workforce and create a more inclusive and vibrant workplace environment.

Setting the Stage for Minority Leadership Development

Recognition of systemic barriers: Examining the historical context helps us recognize the deep-rooted systemic obstacles that have historically limited the representation of marginalized communities in leadership positions. It allows us to understand how specific groups have been systematically excluded or marginalized due to discriminatory practices, biases, and unequal power structures.

Addressing inequality: By understanding the historical context, we can gain insight into the persistent patterns of inequality and the specific challenges marginalized communities face in accessing leadership roles. This knowledge is crucial for developing effective strategies and policies to address and overcome these barriers, promoting diversity, and fostering inclusion.

Empowering marginalized communities: Historical context provides a foundation for empowering marginalized communities by acknowledging their struggles and achievements. It helps validate their experiences and aspirations, enabling individuals from these communities to take pride in their heritage, culture, and contributions. Understanding the historical context can inspire collective action, confidence, and resilience within marginalized communities.

Informing inclusive leadership practices: By examining historical patterns, we can learn from the successes and failures of past efforts to promote minority leadership. This knowledge can inform the development of inclusive leadership practices that address marginalized communities' unique needs and perspectives. It enables organizations and institutions to create environments that support diverse leadership and promote equity and social justice.

Reducing bias and stereotypes: Historical context can help challenge and dispel stereotypes and biases that have hindered the advancement of marginalized communities. Understanding the historical factors contributing to underrepresentation can counteract these biases and promote fairer evaluations of leadership potential. Understanding historical factors can also lead to more equitable opportunities for individuals from marginalized communities to assume leadership roles.

Building a more inclusive society: Insights from the historical context of underrepresentation and marginalization in minority leadership is essential for building a more inclusive community. It encourages us to critically examine existing power structures, systems, and policies and work towards dismantling the barriers perpetuating inequality. By embracing diversity and inclusion in leadership positions, we can harness the full potential of all individuals, foster social cohesion, and create a more just and equitable society.

Uncovering root causes: Examining the historical context helps us identify the root causes of underrepresentation and marginalization. It allows us to trace the historical patterns of discrimination, exclusion, and systemic biases that have shaped the current landscape. By understanding these root causes, we can implement targeted interventions and policies to address them effectively.

Recognizing intersectionality: Historical context highlights the intersectionality of identities and experiences within marginalized communities. It emphasizes that individuals may face multiple forms of marginalization based on race, gender, sexuality, disability, or socioeconomic status. Understanding this intersectionality is crucial for developing comprehensive approaches that consider the unique challenges faced by different groups and promote inclusive leadership across various dimensions.

Fostering social cohesion: By understanding the historical context, we can promote social cohesion by bridging gaps in understanding and empathy. It enables individuals from different backgrounds to develop a deeper appreciation for the struggles and triumphs of marginalized communities. This understanding can increase solidarity, support, and collaboration, strengthening social bonds and creating a more harmonious and cohesive society.

Encouraging inclusive policy-making: Historical context guides policy-making that promotes diversity and inclusion in leadership. It informs the development of affirmative action initiatives, diversity quotas, mentorship programs, and other strategies aimed at addressing historical imbalances. By grounding policies in historical knowledge, decision-makers can better anticipate potential challenges and design interventions that are responsive to the specific needs of marginalized communities.

Empathy and allyship: Knowing historical context cultivates empathy and fosters allyship among individuals outside marginalized communities. It provides insights into the struggles and discrimination faced by these communities over time. This empathy can drive individuals to become active allies, advocating for more excellent representation and supporting initiatives that challenge systemic barriers to minority leadership.

Avoiding historical repetition: By studying the historical context, we can learn from past mistakes and avoid perpetuating patterns of underrepresentation and marginalization. It serves as a reminder of the consequences of exclusionary practices and biased decision-making. This knowledge prompts individuals and organizations to actively seek change, challenge norms, and implement strategies that break free from historical cycles of inequality.

Knowing the historical context of underrepresentation and marginalization in minority leadership provides:

- Valuable insights for addressing inequality.

- Empowering marginalized communities.
- Informing inclusive leadership practices.
- Reducing bias and stereotypes.
- Building a more inclusive society.

In summary, comprehending the historical context of underrepresentation and marginalization in minority leadership is critical for uncovering root causes, recognizing intersectionality, fostering social cohesion, informing policymaking, cultivating empathy and allyship, and avoiding historical repetition. By acknowledging and addressing historical injustices, we can work towards creating a more equitable and inclusive society that uplifts and celebrates the leadership potential of all individuals, regardless of their background.

Exploring the Value of Race, Age, and Gender in Leadership

In today's increasingly interconnected and diverse world, understanding the significance of race, age, and gender diversity in leadership development is essential for organizations seeking to thrive in dynamic and inclusive environments. Embracing diversity in leadership not only promotes fairness and social justice but also brings a multitude of valuable benefits. From fostering innovative thinking to enhancing cultural competence, inclusive leadership practices have the power to drive organizational success, tap into untapped talent pools, and create a more equitable society.

In this section, we will explore 15 valuable benefits that arise from race, age, and gender diversity in leadership development. These benefits include diverse perspectives, improved decision-making, enhanced creativity, market insights, and social responsibility. By delving into these points, we will uncover the immense value that embracing diversity in leadership can bring to organizations and society.

Diversity of perspectives: Embracing race, age, and gender diversity in leadership development fosters a broader range of perspectives and experiences. Different racial, generational, and gender identities bring unique insights, cultural backgrounds, and life experiences to organizations. This diversity of perspectives enriches decision-making processes, enhances problem-solving capabilities, and encourages innovative approaches to challenges.

Enhanced creativity and innovation: By including individuals from diverse racial, age, and gender backgrounds in leadership development, organizations can tap into a wider pool of creativity and innovation. Diverse teams bring together varied ways of thinking, problem-solving strategies, and approaches to decision-making. This diversity sparks creativity, encourages the exploration of new ideas, and enables organizations to adapt to a rapidly changing world.

Improved decision-making and problem-solving: When leadership development encompasses diverse racial, age, and gender identities, decision-making and problem-solving processes benefit from including multiple perspectives. Culturally diverse teams are more likely to consider a broader range of options, challenge groupthink, and critically evaluate assumptions.

Organizations benefit from these attributes leading to more robust decision-making, reduced bias, and increased effectiveness in addressing complex challenges.

Broader skill sets and competencies: Embracing diversity in leadership development ensures a more comprehensive range of skills and competencies within an organization. Different racial, age, and gender identities often bring varied professional backgrounds, expertise, and strengths. This diversity of skills can enhance the collective capabilities of leadership teams, promoting a more well-rounded approach to organizational goals and challenges.

Increased employee engagement and morale: When individuals from diverse racial, age, and gender backgrounds have access to opportunities for leadership development, it sends a message of inclusivity and fairness within the organization. This access leads to increased employee engagement, morale, and satisfaction. Employees feel valued, represented, and motivated to contribute their best, knowing their organization respects and appreciates their diverse identities and perspectives.

Expanded market reach and customer understanding: A diverse leadership development approach that includes individuals from different racial, age, and gender backgrounds helps organizations better understand and connect with culturally diverse customer bases. Leadership teams that mirror the diversity of their target markets are more likely to have insights into customer needs, preferences, and cultural nuances. This understanding enhances customer satisfaction, strengthens relationships, and expands market reach.

Role modeling and inspiration: Leadership development incorporating individuals from diverse racial, age, and gender backgrounds is a powerful form of role modeling. When individuals from historically underrepresented groups assume leadership positions, they inspire others within their communities to pursue leadership roles. This representation encourages aspiring leaders from similar backgrounds, breaks stereotypes, and fosters a sense of possibility and empowerment.

Increased adaptability and resilience: Diverse leadership development promotes adaptability and stability in the face of change and adversity. Individuals from diverse racial, age, and gender backgrounds often bring different life experiences and perspectives, which can help organizations navigate complex challenges, seize new opportunities, and effectively respond to a rapidly evolving business landscape.

Improved cultural competence: Leadership development that embraces race, age, and gender diversity enhances cultural competence within organizations. Leaders gain a deeper understanding of cultural norms, values, and practices, allowing them to navigate multicultural environments with sensitivity and respect. This cultural competence fosters more substantial relationships with diverse stakeholders within and outside the organization.

Enhanced employee retention and recruitment: Organizations prioritizing race, age, and gender diversity in leadership development tend to experience improved employee retention and attraction. Inclusive leadership practices create an environment where individuals from all backgrounds feel valued and supported. Inclusive leadership practices foster loyalty, encourage talent retention, and make the organization more attractive to diverse talent-seeking opportunities for growth and advancement.

Expanded market insights and innovation: A diverse leadership development approach brings a deeper understanding of culturally diverse markets and customer segments. Leaders from different racial, age, and gender backgrounds can identify emerging trends, consumer preferences, and unmet needs within specific demographic groups. This market insight drives innovation, product development, and market expansion strategies that cater to a broader range of customers.

Enhanced reputation and brand image: Organizations prioritizing diversity and inclusivity in leadership development cultivate a positive reputation and brand image. A commitment to diversity sends a solid message to stakeholders, demonstrating an organization's values and commitment to equity. This reputation enhances trust, attracts customers and clients who prioritize diversity, and creates a positive brand image in the eyes of the public.

Mitigation of bias and discrimination: By promoting race, age, and gender diversity in leadership development, organizations actively work to mitigate prejudice and discrimination. Diverse leadership teams can challenge unconscious biases, disrupt stereotypes, and promote fairer decision-making processes. Promoting culturally diverse leadership fosters a more inclusive organizational culture where individuals are evaluated based on their abilities and contributions rather than preconceived notions associated with their race, age, or gender.

Enhanced global perspectives: In an increasingly interconnected world, leadership development practices encompassing diverse racial, age, and gender identities engender a more global perspective within organizations. Leaders with diverse backgrounds can provide insights into international markets, cultural dynamics, and global trends. This global perspective enables organizations to navigate global business environments, forge international partnerships, and capitalize on global opportunities.

Social responsibility and ethical leadership: Embracing race, age, and gender diversity in leadership development aligns with principles of social responsibility and ethical leadership. Organizations that prioritize diversity demonstrate their commitment to creating a more just and equitable society. They become advocates for equal opportunities and contribute to the dismantling of systemic barriers that have historically marginalized certain groups.

Race, age, and gender diversity in leadership development offer valuable benefits such as diverse perspectives, enhanced creativity, and innovation, improved decision-making and problem-solving, broader skill sets and competencies, increased employee engagement and morale, expanded market reach and customer understanding, as well as role modeling and inspiration. Embracing and nurturing these forms of diversity leads to more inclusive and effective leadership, benefiting both organizations and other stakeholders.

The additional benefits, including increased adaptability and resilience, improved cultural competence, enhanced employee retention and recruitment, expanded market insights and innovation, enhanced reputation and brand image, mitigation of bias and discrimination, enhanced global perspectives, and social responsibility, can be leveraged to maximize advantages of diversity, by which organizations can drive positive change, foster inclusive cultures, and achieve tremendous success in a diverse and rapidly evolving world.

Questions for Leadership Discussion

1. How can my/our organization effectively address and overcome systemic barriers that have historically limited the representation of marginalized communities in leadership positions?

2. What strategies can my/our organization implement to foster inclusive leadership practices that promote diversity of perspectives and enhance decision-making, problem-solving, and innovation within their organizations?

3. How can my/our organization ensure that race, age, and gender diversity in leadership development is not just a symbolic gesture but a genuine commitment to social responsibility and ethical leadership?

4. How can organizations shift from tokenistic approaches to harnessing the transformative potential of minority leadership? How might leaders play a pivotal role in creating an environment ensuring that diverse voices are heard, valued, and incorporated into decision-making processes to drive authentic innovation and organizational success?

5. How can organizations effectively communicate these advantages to both internal and external stakeholders? What strategies can organizations employ to not only attract diverse talent but also create a culture of inclusion that enables leaders to thrive and amplify their unique perspectives, ultimately contributing to enhanced creativity, adaptability, and improved overall organizational performance?

CHAPTER TWO

The Changing Landscape: Shifting Perspectives on Diversity and Inclusion

"

Diverse leadership teams bring numerous benefits in terms of shifting perspectives on diversity and inclusion for minority leaders...

The evolution of diversity and inclusion in organizations is marked by milestones and societal shifts, reflecting the growing recognition that diversity is a matter of compliance and strategic advantage. From the initial focus on equal employment opportunities to the broader emphasis on inclusivity and belonging, organizations have come to understand the transformative power of diversity in driving innovation, enhancing decision-making, and fostering a positive organizational culture. As we delve into the specific periods of this evolution, it becomes evident that the quest for diversity and inclusion is an ongoing process, demanding continuous learning, adaptation, and a commitment to creating environments that empower all individuals to thrive and contribute their unique perspectives.

Over the past six decades, organizations' diversity and inclusion landscape has undergone a significant transformation. From the passage of key legislation, including the 1964 Civil Rights

Act, to shifting social and cultural norms, diversity and inclusion initiatives have evolved by changing perspectives, social movements, and recognizing the value diverse voices bring. This journey encompasses milestones, policy changes, and strategic shifts that have propelled organizations toward creating more inclusive workplaces.

The Evolution of Diversity and Inclusion in Organizations

Here we will explore the evolution of diversity and inclusion in organizations from 1964 to 2021, highlighting key developments and trends shaping the path toward equity, representation, and social change. Examining these six defining periods allows us to gain insights into the progress, challenges, and ongoing work necessary to foster diverse and inclusive organizational cultures.

1964-1980: The Civil Rights Act of 1964, a landmark legislation in the United States, marked a turning point in the evolution of diversity and inclusion in organizations. It prohibited discrimination based on race, color, religion, sex, or national origin. This act prompted organizations to address discriminatory practices and take initial steps toward inclusivity. The U.S. government implemented Affirmative action policies to promote equal employment opportunities for underrepresented groups, particularly in government and federally funded organizations.

1980-2000: During this period, diversity and inclusion began to gain more attention in organizational settings. The concept expanded beyond legal compliance, with organizations recognizing the value of diverse perspectives and experiences. Workforce demographics changed, and businesses realized that inclusive practices could enhance innovation, customer satisfaction, and overall performance. Employee resource groups and diversity councils emerged as platforms for underrepresented groups to voice their concerns and contribute to organizational decision-making and policies.

2000-2010: The early 2000s saw increased efforts to embed diversity and inclusion into organizational cultures. Many companies established diversity and inclusion departments or positions to drive change systematically. Diversity training programs aimed to raise awareness and mitigate bias within the workplace. The business case for diversity and inclusion became more prominent, with studies demonstrating positive correlations between diversity, financial performance, and competitive advantage.

2010-2015: This period shifted towards a more strategic and holistic approach to diversity and inclusion. Organizations began focusing on creating inclusive cultures where individuals from all backgrounds could thrive. They recognized the importance of psychological safety, belonging, and respect as critical components of inclusive workplaces. The U.S. Department of Labor implemented diversity metrics and accountability measures to track progress and hold organizations accountable for creating equitable opportunities for all employees.

2016-2020: Diversity and inclusion efforts faced renewed attention and urgency in this period. Social movements like

#MeToo and Black Lives Matter highlighted the ongoing challenges faced by marginalized groups and prompted organizations to reevaluate their commitment to diversity and inclusion. Diversity, equity, and inclusion (DEI) initiatives expanded beyond gender and racial diversity to encompass a broader range of identities, including LGBTQ+ individuals, people with disabilities, and individuals from diverse socioeconomic backgrounds.

2021-Present: 2021 witnessed a heightened focus on diversity, equity, and inclusion. Organizations increasingly acknowledged the need for systemic change and accountability. Calls for transparency, representation, and anti-racist practices became louder. Diversity and inclusion efforts evolved to prioritize equity, aiming to address systemic barriers and create fair and just workplaces. There was an increased emphasis on intersectionality, recognizing the unique experiences and challenges faced by individuals with multiple marginalized identities.

However, it is worth noting that in 2023, the Supreme Court made a significant affirmative action ruling that impacted diversity and inclusion efforts in higher education. The ruling reversed the constitutionality of affirmative action, which allowed universities to consider race as a factor in admissions decisions to promote diversity. This decision highlights the ongoing legal and societal debates surrounding affirmative action. It also underscores the importance of ongoing efforts to create inclusive environments that value diverse perspectives and promote equal opportunities for all.

Throughout the decades, the evolution of diversity and inclusion in organizations has moved beyond legal compliance to encompass strategic initiatives, cultural transformation, and social justice aspirations. The journey continues as organizations strive to create truly inclusive environments where all individuals, regardless of their backgrounds, can thrive and contribute to their fullest potential.

Identifying the Challenges of Minority Leaders

Identifying the challenges of minority leaders in terms of shifting perspectives on diversity and inclusion requires an understanding of the complex dynamics and evolving nature of diversity efforts. While progress in cultural diversity amongst leadership ranks within organizations is evident, significant challenges persist that hinder the advancement of minority leaders. Here are nine key challenges minority leaders face in the context of shifting perspectives on diversity and inclusion:

Tokenism and Symbolic Diversity: In the complex landscape of minority leadership, a shadow often lurks – one that comes in the form of tokenism and symbolic diversity. In this narrative, minority leaders find themselves navigating treacherous waters, where their ascent to leadership positions seems to be fueled by external agendas rather than their true potential. Tokenism, a term etched in the struggle for genuine inclusivity, portrays a scenario where these leaders are appointed or promoted not for their skills, expertise, or merit but rather to meet predefined diversity quotas or to present an illusion of embracing diversity.

This precarious challenge places minority leaders in a bind. On the one hand, they obtain leadership positions, which could signal a step toward progress. Yet, on closer inspection, the foundation is shaky, for their credibility becomes ensnared in the web of tokenism. The danger emerges when their accomplishments and contributions become overshadowed by the suspicion that they are there merely as representatives of their identity group. The achievements that should have a direct attribution to their qualifications, experience, and skill set can quickly become misconstrued as products of their ethnicity, gender, or other defining traits.

This dichotomy tears at the fabric of their leadership journey. The struggle becomes twofold: the challenge to prove oneself as a capable leader while simultaneously debunking the notion that their position is solely a product of symbolic diversity. The insidious whisper taints their success that they are there not for their capabilities but as a checkbox to fulfill an agenda. This not only hampers their individual growth and potential but also erodes the very foundation of genuine diversity and inclusivity.

Tokenism and symbolic diversity thus serve as poignant reminders of the uphill battle that minority leaders often face. The struggle to navigate this maze requires a delicate balance of self-assurance, resilience, and the fierce determination to transcend the imposed limitations and stand as a testament to their true potential.

Implicit Bias and Stereotyping: In the intricate dance of leadership dynamics, minority leaders often confront a silent adversary that goes by many names: implicit bias and stereotyping. These subtle forces wield significant power, casting long shadows upon the path of those who aspire to lead. At its heart lies a challenge that stems from the historical roots of our social fabric – networks woven over time, predominantly composed of individuals who belong to the majority groups.

Implicit bias, like an unseen current, shapes perceptions and attitudes even in the most well-intentioned minds. It's the whispers of assumptions that reverberate louder than we realize. These biases paint a picture that is often far from the truth – one where specific individuals appear to be more fitting, more familiar, or deserving of leadership roles based solely on factors like ethnicity, gender, or cultural background. Such biases subtly nudge minority leaders to the fringes, obscuring their potential and relegating them to roles that fall short of their true capabilities.

Coupled with implicit bias is the powerful phenomenon of stereotyping. Like well-worn scripts, stereotypes cast minority leaders into predefined roles, constraining their identities within a narrow frame. Stereotyping erases their individuality and sidelines their unique skills and insights. As they strive to ascend the leadership ladder, these leaders often find their path obstructed by preconceived notions, making it an uphill battle to shatter these molds and redefine their narrative.

The implications of this challenge are profound. Networks, often formed naturally through shared experiences and affiliations, hold immense sway in the realm of leadership opportunities. The historical skew towards majority-group networks means that minority leaders must contend with not just climbing the ladder, but also constructing their scaffolding of connections. This task requires extra effort, persistence, and sometimes defying ingrained biases.

The absence of diverse mentorship and sponsorship amplifies this struggle. Lacking role models who reflect their own identities and experiences, minority leaders are denied the crucial guidance and advocacy that can accelerate their growth. This deficiency in meaningful mentorship can be a significant barrier to unlocking their full potential and can perpetuate the underrepresentation cycle.

Implicit bias and stereotyping thus underscore the dire need for systemic change. Overcoming these challenges demands collective introspection, redefining norms, and recognizing every leader's inherent worth and potential, regardless of their background. It requires weaving a new fabric of networks that reflects the authentic tapestry of diversity. Only then can minority leaders rise unhindered, their potential fully realized, and their impact unbounded.

Limited Access to Networks and Mentors: In the complicated leadership landscape, a profound challenge often stands as a formidable hurdle in the path of minority leaders – the challenge of limited access to networks and mentors. It's a challenge born of history that echoes the patterns of exclusion and inequality that have persisted for generations. At its core lies a stark reality: the networks that wield influence and open doors have, over time, been molded in the image of majority groups.

Imagine a vast labyrinth of connections, a complex web spun through shared experiences, affiliations, and social circles. Often unspoken and informal, these networks are the conduits through which opportunities flow. They are the bridges to mentorship, guidance, and sponsorship – pillars that can propel leaders forward. Yet, for minority leaders, these bridges can be precarious; some even appear inaccessible.

Historical networks have often grown organically, built upon shared experiences and cultural affinities. They've evolved by the communities that formed them, influenced by the perspectives of the dominant culture. Over time, this has led to networks predominantly comprising individuals from majority groups. It's not a matter of overt exclusion but rather a silent perpetuation of existing power dynamics.

The implications of this network imbalance are far-reaching. The exclusion of minority leaders into influential networks results in missing insights, opportunities, and connections these networks offer. Access to mentors – experienced guides who can offer wisdom, advocate for growth, and provide a roadmap – becomes challenging. And sponsorship, a vital form of support that can elevate careers to new heights, remains elusive.

Without diverse mentors who understand the unique challenges faced by minority leaders, misguidance or lack thereof can stunt professional growth. A mentor's guidance, shaped by shared experiences, can be particularly impactful in navigating the complexities of leadership. Yet, when the mentorship landscape is homogenous, it perpetuates a cycle of unequal access to opportunities, making it harder for minority leaders to break through glass ceilings.

The solution, then, lies not in dismantling existing networks but in enriching them. It requires acknowledging the implicit biases that have shaped these networks and actively working to reshape them. It necessitates creating spaces where mentorship transcends cultural boundaries, where sponsorship isn't reserved for those who fit a specific mold. It's about recognizing that diversity in networks and mentorship isn't just an ethical imperative; it's a strategic one that unleashes untapped potential.

In the global socioeconomic culture, where diversity is an asset, where unique perspectives spark innovation and drive progress, it's essential to bridge this gap. As we forge connections that bridge the divides of history, we unlock the full spectrum of leadership potential. We weave a tapestry of networks and mentors that reflect the rich diversity of our society, enabling every leader – regardless of their background – to thrive and lead with their full capabilities.

Inadequate Organizational Support: In the complex ecosystem of organizational dynamics, a stark reality often emerges – the challenge of inadequate support for minority leaders. It's a challenge reverberating through the corridors of power and underscores the urgent need for a shift in organizational paradigms. At its heart lies a critical imbalance – the absence of robust support systems and resources that can empower minority leaders to surmount their unique hurdles.

Imagine an organization as a vessel embarking on a journey toward innovation, growth, and success. Its crew, comprised of leaders and employees, navigates the tumultuous waters of the business landscape. For minority leaders, this journey can be particularly arduous, marked by a distinct set of challenges and uncertainties. Yet, without the correct provisions, this voyage becomes even more perilous.

At the helm of an organization's support structure should be a suite of initiatives designed to nurture leadership potential. Leadership development programs – those transformative platforms that equip leaders with skills, insights, and strategies – can be a lifeline for minority leaders. However, the reality is often different. These programs may find themselves insufficient to address the nuanced challenges faced by minority leaders, leaving them navigating uncharted waters without a compass.

Mentorship, too, is a beacon of guidance that can illuminate the path to success. Yet, for minority leaders, this guiding light may flicker. The absence of diverse mentors who comprehend their unique struggles and aspirations can lead to feelings of isolation. When not inclusive, mentorship initiatives inadvertently reinforce the notion that success is meant for a select few, leaving minority leaders searching for a foothold in the organizational ascent.

Inclusive policies are the very bedrock of an equitable organizational culture. They send a resounding message that every voice matters and that every leader's potential is recognized and nurtured. However, when such policies are absent or poorly executed, minority leaders are left grappling with an unsettling truth – their contributions may be undervalued, their perspectives marginalized.

Without these pillars of support – development programs, mentorship initiatives, and inclusive policies – minority leaders can find their journeys mired in frustration. Their career paths may become stymied by barriers that their counterparts do not encounter. Their unique talents may go untapped, their contributions untended. The absence of support can create a sense of disillusionment, eroding the fabric of organizational engagement and commitment.

The solution lies in redefining the organizational infrastructure, infusing it with inclusivity and intentionality. It requires recognizing that the challenges faced by minority leaders are not isolated incidents but systemic issues that require systemic solutions. Organizations must invest in leadership development programs that are attuned to the needs of all leaders, regardless of their background. They must foster mentorship networks that reflect the diversity of their workforce, providing every leader with the support they deserve.

Inclusive policies must be the cornerstone, enshrining the principles of fairness, equal opportunity, and recognition of diverse contributions. Organizations that embark on this transformational journey unlock a world of potential – a world where minority leaders are not just survivors but thrivers, where their ascent is not impeded by obstacles but facilitated by the wind of collective support. It's a world where every leader, regardless of their background, is poised to sail the seas of success with confidence, purpose, and the backing of an organization that truly values their leadership.

Microaggressions and Discrimination: Picture a workplace as a mosaic of diverse talents, each piece contributing to the grand tapestry of an organization's success. Amid this intricate pattern, minority leaders navigate a landscape that often bears the burden of a painful truth – the prevalence of microaggressions and overt discrimination. These insidious forces cast a shadow over the workplace environment, leading to a host of negative consequences that ripple through both the individual and the organization.

Microaggressions, those subtle and often unintentional slights or comments, can create a minefield of emotional hurdles for minority leaders. Imagine a leader giving their all, contributing their expertise, only to be met with words that subtly question their qualifications or imply that they are an exception to the norm. These seemingly innocuous remarks, while appearing harmless on the surface, are like pebbles that, when piled, become a heavy burden. They accumulate over time, eroding the leader's self-assurance and gnawing at their confidence.

Overt discrimination, on the other hand, casts a far darker shadow. It's the harsh glare of bias and prejudice, one that leaves no room for subtlety. Imagine a leader's achievements being overshadowed by their identity – their race, gender, ethnicity, or any other characteristic that should have no bearing on their professional prowess. This form of discrimination chips away at the leader's self-esteem and creates a sense of hostility in the workplace. The result is an environment where the very act of contributing becomes an uphill battle.

The effects of these experiences are far-reaching. Imagine a leader who, once brimming with ideas and energy, begins to second-guess their abilities. Microaggressions and discrimination create an environment where they feel their contributions are continually under scrutiny, fostering self-doubt and hesitancy. The emotional toll can be profound, leading to burnout and isolation.

Moreover, when these experiences are allowed to persist, they disrupt the delicate balance of teamwork and collaboration. An organization is built on trust, mutual respect, and the collective pursuit of goals. However, when minority leaders face microaggressions and discrimination, this foundation is undermined. Colleagues and team members may hesitate to collaborate with someone they perceive is not treated fairly, leading to fractured relationships and a less cohesive workforce.

Career advancement, a vital aspect of professional growth, can also be hindered by these challenges. Imagine a leader striving for higher positions, only to encounter barriers that seem insurmountable due to their identity. Microaggressions and discrimination, when unchecked, can lead to fewer opportunities and less recognition, stifling upward mobility.

Yet, the path forward is not one of resignation but of transformation. Organizations must recognize that eradicating microaggressions and discrimination requires a concerted effort. Training programs that sensitize employees to the impact of their words and actions can be the first step toward change. Open dialogues and safe spaces enable leaders to share their experiences and allies to become advocates for equality.

By creating an environment that not only condemns discrimination but actively cultivates inclusivity, organizations can harness the full potential of their minority leaders. Imagine a workplace where every leader, regardless of their background, can bring their whole selves to work – unburdened by the weight of microaggressions, unencumbered by the shackles of discrimination. It's a world where contributions are valued based on merit, and leadership flourishes in an atmosphere of respect, empowerment, and authentic diversity.

Cultural Expectations and Stereotype Threat: Imagine standing at the intersection of your professional aspirations and the cultural expectations surrounding you. For minority leaders, this juncture can be a complex battleground, where the pressure to disprove stereotypes becomes a weighty burden. This phenomenon is known as stereotype threat – a psychological challenge that can hinder the fullest expression of skills and talents.

Consider a minority leader navigating the delicate balance between their identity and leadership demands. They face the expectation to excel in their role and defy ingrained stereotypes that society has associated with their racial, ethnic, or gender background. Imagine a woman leading and striving to showcase her decisiveness in a world where stereotypes often label her indecisive. Or a leader of color aiming to display his analytical prowess in a realm where the stereotype of his group might be deemed less analytical.

This constant pressure to outperform these stereotypes creates a cognitive dissonance that can affect performance and well-being. Imagine being keenly aware that your actions are being evaluated through the lens of preconceived notions. The result is a heightened sense of anxiety – a fear of confirming the very stereotypes you aim to dismantle. This anxiety not only hampers creativity and innovation but can also lead to a phenomenon called "stereotype lift," where an individual from a non-minority group may be given an advantage simply due to lower expectations associated with stereotypes.

Picture a leader who, under this weight of stereotype threat, may feel compelled to prove their competence repeatedly. The exhaustion accompanying this effort can leave them drained, impacting their effectiveness. This additional stress can chip away at self-confidence and detract from their ability to make impactful decisions. It's as if they are constantly juggling two roles – that of a leader and that of a cultural ambassador, trying to reconcile societal expectations with their authentic selves.

Yet, just as stereotype threat can be a challenge, it also holds the seed of transformation. Imagine a world where these expectations are dismantled, and leaders are assessed solely on their abilities. Organizations have the power to create environments where individuals are empowered to challenge stereotypes without the fear of confirmation bias. Transformation begins with acknowledging and confronting these biases head-on, fostering a culture of inclusivity, and celebrating the unique contributions of all leaders.

Leadership is not about fitting into predefined molds but embracing diverse perspectives, breaking free from limiting expectations and setting new standards. Imagine a world where minority leaders can fully leverage their skills and capabilities, unburdened by stereotype threat. It's a world where they can lead authentically, inspire innovation, and confidently navigate challenges. By recognizing and dismantling the shackles of stereotype threat, organizations can unleash all their leaders' potential, forging a path toward greater diversity, inclusion, and excellence.

Lack of Representation and Role Models: In leadership, the absence of representation can cast a long shadow over the aspirations of emerging minority leaders. Imagine a young professional of color, brimming with potential but faced with a scarcity of role models who mirror their background and experiences at the helm of influential positions. This vacuum of visible representation can be a daunting hurdle, robbing them of a vital source of inspiration and guidance.

Think about the impact of having no one who shares your journey, no one who can offer insights drawn from a similar narrative. For emerging minority leaders, the lack of relatable role models can translate into uncertainty about their career trajectories. Without visible success stories illuminating the path ahead, their sense of belonging within the leadership realm may falter. It's akin to navigating uncharted waters without a compass or a map.

Consider how representation plays a pivotal role in shaping aspirations. When young minds observe leaders who share their ethnicity, gender, or cultural heritage breaking new ground, a sense of possibility takes root. These role models become beacons, illuminating the way forward and dispelling doubts. Witnessing someone who looks like they thrive at the highest echelons of leadership can solidify the belief that their ambitions are achievable, that they, too, can overcome barriers and ascend to positions of influence.

Nevertheless, the absence of such role models leaves a void that can inadvertently perpetuate the cycle of underrepresentation. Without diverse leaders blazing trails and demonstrating that success transcends stereotypes, minority talents might remain untapped. The result is a missed opportunity for organizations to harness a wealth of innovative perspectives and fresh approaches that minority leaders can bring.

To bridge this gap, organizations must recognize the power of representation in shaping the aspirations of the next generation.

They must be intentional about spotlighting the accomplishments of minority leaders, making their journeys visible and accessible. By fostering mentorship programs, networking opportunities, and platforms for sharing experiences, organizations can cultivate an environment where emerging minority leaders find role models and forge connections that nurture their growth.

It is possible to envision the impact of a landscape where every aspiring minority leader has a trailblazer to look up to, where they can see their potential reflected in the stories of those who have walked the path before them. This tapestry of representation weaves together the threads of inspiration, aspiration, and belonging, empowering emerging leaders to rise with confidence and organizations to harness the full spectrum of talent that diversity offers. It's a vision where representation becomes a catalyst for transformation, building bridges across generations and forging a more inclusive and impactful future of leadership.

Intersectionality and Multiple Identities: In the intricate tapestry of diversity, intersectionality emerges as a profound truth that shapes the experiences of minority leaders with multiple marginalized identities. Picture a leader who navigates the terrain of being a person of color and grapples with the complexities of gender, sexuality, disability, or ethnicity. Each identity carries its challenges, and when these facets intersect, a unique and often compounded set of hurdles emerges.

Consider a woman of color who is in a leadership role. She is not just contending with racial biases but also with the gender-related prejudices that women often face. Moreover, her ethnicity and cultural background introduce another layer of potential discrimination. Her leadership journey becomes a tightrope walk where she must simultaneously address these facets of her identity while striving to lead authentically and confidently.

This intersectionality of identities magnifies the intricacies of systemic biases. It's like navigating a maze with walls that shift and change based on the multitude of identities one embodies. The challenges this woman of color face are not isolated; they intertwine in ways that demand her attention, resilience, and ability to navigate a landscape riddled with stereotypes and prejudices.

Enter the concept of codeswitching—a linguistic and behavioral adaptation often used by individuals with intersecting identities. Our woman of color leader may code-switch between different social contexts. She may emphasize her racial identity in one setting to align with the majority culture's expectations. In another, she may downplay her cultural ethnicity to avoid potential discrimination. This dynamic juggling act is a survival strategy to navigate the complexities of intersecting identities in a world that may not fully embrace them all.

However, codeswitching comes at a cost. The energy spent adapting to different expectations detracts from channeling that energy into leadership endeavors. It's an extra layer of cognitive load that majority leaders often do not have to bear. For minority leaders with intersecting identities, the delicate balance between authenticity and fitting into societal norms can be exhausting, affecting their well-being and ability to lead effectively.

To create an environment where intersectional minority leaders can thrive, organizations must acknowledge these compound challenges. They must provide spaces that allow leaders to bring their whole selves to work, free from the constraints of codeswitching. Diversity and inclusion initiatives must address the multifaceted nature of identity, recognizing that the struggles of an individual can't be compartmentalized. Instead, they interweave into a complex tapestry, one that, when embraced and celebrated, enriches the leadership landscape with perspectives that defy simplistic categorizations.

It is possible to create an environment where intersectional minority leaders can rise without the burden of navigating intersecting biases, where their leadership is celebrated for the unique tapestry of experiences they bring. It's an environment where the organization recognizes that true diversity goes beyond quotas—it's about fostering an environment where every individual can thrive authentically, regardless of the intricate interplay of their identities.

Resistance to Change and Bias in Decision-Making: In the ever-changing landscape of diversity and inclusion, the inertia of resistance to change remains a formidable obstacle. Despite the gradual evolution of perspectives, biases can linger in the very fibers of decision-making processes within organizations. Imagine a boardroom where promotions and resource allocation decisions occur. Unconscious biases, often deeply ingrained and subtle, can unconsciously influence these pivotal choices. These biases can perpetuate inequitable outcomes for minority leaders, who find themselves navigating a landscape where these hidden prejudices might overshadow their potential and qualifications.

To break free from these patterns, organizations must confront the systemic barriers that enable biases to persist. The challenge lies in dismantling established norms and practices perpetuating these inequities. It's about recognizing that change requires more than surface-level efforts; it demands an internal restructuring that reshapes the very foundations of decision-making processes.

The journey toward unbiased decision-making encompasses various dimensions. It involves embedding inclusive practices at every organizational level, from the initial recruitment stages to leadership development programs. Envision a professional environment where job postings are worded in ways that attract a diverse pool of candidates, where interview panels are consciously composed to include varied perspectives, and where promotion criteria are rigorously examined for potential bias. This vision necessitates an intentional effort to recalibrate organizational DNA.

Additionally, suppose an organization is committed to fostering a continual learning and growth culture, where employees are educated about unconscious biases and given the tools to mitigate them. This process would require individual introspection and collective responsibility. By shining a light on these biases and taking concrete steps to challenge them; organizations pave the way for equitable decision-making processes.

The potential rewards of such efforts are immense. Picture a scenario where minority leaders are genuinely empowered to rise based on their skills and qualifications, unencumbered by the weight of implicit biases. This transformation isn't just about ticking boxes on a diversity checklist; it's about realizing the untapped potential of leaders who bring unique perspectives to the organization. It's about embracing diversity not as a buzzword, but as a strategic advantage that propels organizations into a future marked by innovation and growth.

By confronting resistance to change and biases in decision-making head-on, organizations embark on a journey toward a truly inclusive and equitable environment. This journey is not without challenges, but it holds the promise of a workplace where every individual—regardless of background—can thrive, contribute, and lead authentically. It's about creating a legacy that shatters the glass ceiling for minority leaders and, in doing so, reshapes the trajectory of leadership for generations to come.

Highlighting the benefits of diverse leadership teams

Shifting perspectives on diversity and inclusion have propelled organizations to recognize the immense value of diverse leadership teams. Embracing diversity at the highest levels of leadership not only reflects a commitment to equity but also brings a myriad of benefits. In this discussion, we will explore five key benefits that diverse leadership teams offer in shifting perspectives on diversity and inclusion for minority leaders. These benefits include an expanded range of views and ideas, enhanced decision-making and problem-solving, improved cultural competence and sensitivity, increased employee engagement and retention, and an enhanced organizational reputation and innovation.

Examining these benefits helps us to uncover and unlock the transformative power of diverse leadership teams and their contribution to fostering inclusive cultures that empower and amplify the voices of minority leaders. Culturally diverse leadership teams bring numerous benefits in shifting perspectives on diversity and inclusion for minority leaders. Here are five key benefits:

Expanded Range of Perspectives and Ideas: Diverse leadership teams encompass individuals from various racial, ethnic, gender, and cultural backgrounds. This diversity of perspectives enables a broader range of ideas, insights, and problem-solving approaches. Minority leaders, with their unique experiences and viewpoints, contribute fresh perspectives that challenge groupthink and stimulate innovative thinking within the team.

Enhanced Decision-Making and Problem-Solving: Diverse leadership teams are more adept at making well-informed decisions. By considering diverse perspectives, these teams can identify areas of opportunity, mitigate biases, and make more comprehensive and balanced decisions. Including minority leaders help prevent the echo chamber effect and fosters a culture of critical thinking and constructive dialogue.

Improved Cultural Competence and Sensitivity: Diversity in leadership teams enhances cultural competence and sensitivity. Minority leaders bring a firsthand understanding of cultural norms, practices, and nuances, enabling organizations to navigate diverse markets and cater to a wide range of customers and stakeholders. Their insights help develop culturally inclusive strategies that resonate with diverse audiences and foster meaningful connections.

Increased Employee Engagement and Retention: Diverse leadership teams contribute to higher employee engagement and retention levels, particularly among minority employees. When individuals from underrepresented groups see leaders who share their identities, it creates a sense of belonging, inspires confidence, and promotes career aspirations. This representation and inclusivity foster an inclusive organizational culture, attracting and retaining diverse talent.

Enhanced Organizational Reputation and Innovation: Organizations with diverse leadership teams demonstrate a commitment to equity and inclusion, positively impacting their reputation and brand image. They present a progressive, socially responsible organization, attractive to customers, employees, and partners who value diversity. Additionally, diverse leadership teams fuel innovation by fostering a culture of creativity, adaptability, and open-mindedness, leading to new ideas, approaches, and market opportunities.

These benefits emphasize the significance of diverse leadership teams in shifting perspectives on diversity and inclusion. By embracing diversity at the leadership level, organizations can tap into the advantages of multiple perspectives, drive inclusive decision-making, improve cultural competence, engage and retain talent, and enhance their overall reputation and innovative capabilities.

Questions for leadership discussion

1. How can my/our organization overcome tokenism and ensure that minority leaders are valued for their qualifications and skills rather than being perceived as mere symbols of diversity?

2. What strategies can my/our organization implement to mitigate implicit biases and stereotypes that affect the perceptions and opportunities available to minority leaders?

3. How can my/our organization proactively address the limited access of minority leaders to influential networks and mentors, ensuring they have equal opportunities for career growth and development?

CHAPTER THREE

The Power of Identity: Embracing Authentic Leadership

> **"**
>
> *At the core of authentic leadership lies the recognition and embrace of personal identity. When organizations and leaders honor their authentic selves, they create a space for others to do the same, fostering a culture of inclusivity and empowerment.*

In a world that celebrates individuality and recognizes the value of diverse perspectives, embracing authentic leadership has emerged as a powerful force for driving positive change and fostering inclusive environments. This chapter delves into the transformative potential of embracing one's identity as a cornerstone of authentic leadership. We explore how leaders who embrace unique identities, including race, gender, ethnicity, and other dimensions, can unleash the full potential of culturally diverse leadership environments, inspire others, and create meaningful impact within their organizations. By embracing authenticity, leaders can navigate the complexities of their identities, build genuine connections, and forge inclusive cultures that celebrate the richness of diversity. Through this exploration, we uncover the profound power of identity in shaping leadership and driving organizational success.

Unveiling the Intersectionality of Identity in Leadership

Today's globally diverse and interconnected world requires the fundamental capacity to recognize and understand the intersectionality of identity in leadership. Intersectionality acknowledges that individuals possess multiple dimensions of identity that intersect and shape their experiences, perspectives, and challenges. In this exploration, we unveil identity's intricate and interconnected nature, shedding light on how intersectionality influences leadership and its profound impact on organizational success. Though complex and often in-depth, this understanding creates a foundation for building a strong and culturally diverse leadership team within the organization.

The Complexity of Intersectionality: Intersectionality reveals the multifaceted nature of identity by recognizing that individuals may face overlapping systems of discrimination and privilege based on various aspects, such as race, gender, age, sexuality, and disability. This complexity highlights the need to move beyond simplistic categorizations and acknowledge the unique challenges and strengths that arise from the convergence of different identities. Understanding intersectionality in leadership enables organizations to appreciate the richness of diversity and create inclusive spaces that honor and uplift the lived experiences of all individuals.

This mosaic of identities is not just a theoretical construct; it shapes our daily experiences and interactions. Imagine a person who is both a racial minority and a woman or an individual navigating the challenges of being both LGBTQ+ and disabled. These intersections create a unique landscape where systems of discrimination and privilege crisscross in ways that can be both empowering and challenging.

This complexity calls for a departure from simplistic categorizations. It's about recognizing that everyone's journey is layered, and individual experiences cannot be neatly boxed into predefined labels. It's about acknowledging that being a woman doesn't mean the same thing for every woman, and being a person of color doesn't entail the same experiences for all. The journey toward embracing intersectionality has its challenges. It requires ongoing learning, empathy, and a commitment to dismantling biases that stem from oversimplified notions of identity. But the rewards are immeasurable—a workplace that thrives on the strength of its diversity, where every individual's mosaic contributes to a vibrant, inclusive, and harmonious whole.

Broadening Perspectives and Insights: Embracing intersectionality in leadership is like opening a treasure trove of diverse perspectives and insights. Picture a meeting room where leaders from various backgrounds and walks of life come together, each carrying unique experiences shaped by their intersecting identities. This collective tapestry of identities—race, gender, age, sexuality, and more—creates a dynamic exchange of viewpoints that enriches every discussion and decision.

Consider a team led by an individual who identifies as both a woman and a member of an ethnic minority. This leader brings their professional expertise, a wealth of cultural insights, and life experiences. These insights can be game changers when navigating global markets, understanding customer needs, or developing innovative solutions that resonate with diverse audiences.

When leaders draw from their intersectional identities, the result is a wellspring of innovation. The collision of different worldviews sparks a creative fire that ignites fresh ideas and imaginative problem-solving. It's like having a toolkit filled with varied lenses to examine complex challenges. For instance, a leader who has faced disability-related barriers might approach problem-solving with a unique perspective on accessibility and inclusion.

This infusion of diverse perspectives leads to more robust critical thinking. As leaders grapple with complex issues, they draw on their backgrounds to analyze problems from multiple angles. This multi-dimensional approach challenges assumptions and encourages a more holistic understanding of the situation.

Suppose an organization actively embraces intersectionality across its leadership ranks. The decisions made are not just a result of one-dimensional thinking but rather a convergence of varied viewpoints. This diversity of thought allows the organization to tap into an immeasurable well of ideas, make more informed choices, and remain adaptable in the face of change.

Ultimately, the organization becomes a dynamic ecosystem where innovation flourishes, solutions are more comprehensive, and the needs of a diverse range of stakeholders are better met. By welcoming intersectionality, organizations open doors to a world of possibilities, where the richness of human experiences drives progress and shapes a future that truly resonates with all.

Addressing Systemic Inequities: Dismantling systemic inequities demands an exploration of leadership that transcends the confines of a single dimension. The essence of intersectionality—where identities coalesce—breathes new life into organizational paradigms. Imagine this as an expedition into uncharted waters, guided by leaders who carry the multifaceted treasures of their identities.

As leaders step into their roles with a conscious embrace of their intersectional identities—where race, gender, age, and more converge—they pave the way for a dynamic interplay of experiences and wisdom. These leaders are not merely contributors but architects of change, constructing a bridge between diverse narratives that have long remained unlinked.

This convergence of perspectives is the alchemy that transforms leadership. For instance, a leader who identifies as a woman of color is not limited to her level of professional expertise. She brings the layers of her journey as a woman, her experiences rooted in her cultural heritage, and her insights cultivated by the challenges she's faced. These layers ripple through her decision-making, resulting in a tapestry of nuanced, comprehensive, and inherently innovative solutions.

In this grand narrative, the organization emerges as the beneficiary. The wellspring of innovation that flows from embracing intersectionality is not merely a buzzword; it's a tangible advantage. When leaders deftly wield their unique vantage points, the complex becomes approachable, and the enigmatic unfolds with clarity. The organization gains access to an expanded spectrum of ideas, a kaleidoscope of perspectives that illuminates even the darkest corners of complexity.

This cascade of diverse viewpoints breeds robustness in critical thinking. As leaders engage with intricate challenges, they tap into reservoirs of knowledge shaped by their intersecting identities. The very act of addressing systemic inequities becomes an exercise in empathy and understanding. A transformative process emerges, where the leadership journey becomes an odyssey, and the stars of intersectionality guide the voyage toward inclusivity.

As organizations embrace intersectionality, they emerge as vibrant landscapes of potential. The choices made are not mere transactions but the harmonious crescendo of varied voices. With every decision, the organization strides towards a horizon that continually adapts to the changing needs of a diverse array of stakeholders. This journey is not just a narrative of leadership—it is a symphony of transformation, where the once-muted voices harmonize to create a future that resounds with the vibrant hues of intersectionality.

Empowering Underrepresented Leaders: In leadership, intersectionality becomes a radiant beacon of empowerment, illuminating the paths of underrepresented leaders. It's a revelation that resonates deeply, acknowledging the intricate dance of identities and the narratives that flourish within their convergence.

In this context, empowerment emerges as a deliberate act—a journey mapped out by organizations attuned to the symphony of intersecting experiences. As the spotlight shifts to underrepresented leaders, organizations recognize that identity isn't a monolith; it's a kaleidoscope of experiences that shape aspirations, fears, and triumphs.

With this realization, a transformation takes root. Organizations, armed with a nuanced understanding of intersectionality, craft targeted leadership development initiatives. These initiatives are not generic blueprints but personalized journeys that navigate the unique terrain of underrepresented leaders' experiences. As these leaders embark on this path, they're met not with generic advice but tailored guidance that acknowledges their multifaceted identities.

This empowerment is a reservoir of strength—a sanctuary where barriers are addressed head-on. Underrepresented leaders find themselves surrounded by a network that mirrors their journey—a network that speaks their language, understands their struggles, and celebrates their successes. This network isn't a mere construct; it's a lifeline that bridges the gap between aspiration and achievement.

As intersectionality weaves its threads, leaders who have long felt relegated to the shadows rise to prominence. Their voices become amplified, their skills sharpened, and their aspirations nurtured. What blooms is not just a sense of belonging; it's a belief in their capacity to lead and create meaningful change.

This empowerment strikes at the heart of inclusivity, reverberating with the conviction that leadership is not the privilege of a few but the birthright of all. The barriers that once seemed insurmountable crumble and the ceilings that once constrained ambitions shatter. The empowerment that intersectionality ignites isn't merely about participation but transformation.

In this radiant narrative, organizations stand as catalysts of change, understanding that diversity is not a passive state but an active commitment. As underrepresented leaders find their voices amplified and their potential magnified, they become agents of transformation, shaping a future where every identity converges to create a tapestry of leadership brilliance.

Emphasizing the Importance of Embracing Authenticity

In culturally diverse organizations, embracing authenticity must be balanced. Authenticity goes beyond surface-level representation and acknowledges the need for individuals to bring their authentic selves to the workplace. In this exploration, we delve into the significance of embracing authenticity in culturally diverse organizations and how it fosters a sense of belonging, promotes psychological safety, encourages innovation, enhances communication, and drives overall organizational success.

Promoting Psychological Safety: Promoting psychological safety within culturally diverse organizations is essential for creating an environment where all employees can thrive and contribute effectively. Authenticity plays a pivotal role in establishing this psychological safety. When employees are encouraged and supported in being their authentic selves, it creates a space where they can openly express their opinions, ideas, and concerns without fear of negative consequences.

Psychological safety is the foundation of open and honest communication. In an inclusive environment, individuals feel comfortable sharing their viewpoints, even if they differ from the mainstream perspective. This willingness to engage in dialogue and express diverse views enriches discussions and decision-making processes.

One of the remarkable outcomes of psychological safety is its power to encourage risk-taking. When employees know that other members won't dismiss their ideas and their contributions are valued, they are more likely to propose innovative solutions and take calculated risks. This environment empowers employees to step outside their comfort zones, explore new avenues, and experiment with unconventional approaches.

Furthermore, psychological safety encourages collaboration. When employees feel secure in expressing their thoughts, they are more likely to engage in team discussions and brainstorming sessions actively. This collaborative spirit enhances the exchange of ideas and fosters a sense of shared ownership in projects and initiatives.

Importantly, psychological safety in culturally diverse organizations addresses the concerns of individuals who might hesitate to voice their opinions due to potential bias or discrimination. When these employees feel safe and supported, they are more likely to contribute their unique insights, which challenge conventional thinking and lead to innovative solutions.

Promoting psychological safety within a diverse context benefits employees and the organization. It creates an environment where innovation and creativity thrive, and collaboration and effective problem-solving become natural outcomes. By valuing authenticity and fostering a culture of respect and open communication, organizations can nurture psychological safety and reap the rewards of a truly inclusive workplace.

Enhancing Communication and Collaboration: Authenticity is a powerful catalyst for enhancing communication and collaboration within culturally diverse organizations. When employees are encouraged and empowered to express themselves authentically, it creates an environment where communication becomes more genuine, meaningful, and productive.

Open dialogue is a cornerstone of effective communication. Authenticity encourages individuals to share their thoughts, experiences, and viewpoints openly. This willingness to speak openly creates opportunities for deeper discussions as individuals engage in conversations beyond surface-level interactions. By allowing employees to bring their whole selves to the table, organizations tap into diverse perspectives that enrich the quality of conversations and decision-making processes.

Authentic communication also promotes active listening and learning. When individuals express themselves authentically, others are more inclined to listen and understand their viewpoints genuinely. This willingness to listen and learn from different experiences leads to a more inclusive exchange of ideas and knowledge. As a result, employees can broaden their horizons, challenge their assumptions, and develop a deeper understanding of the diverse worldviews present within the organization.

Collaboration thrives in environments where diverse perspectives are valued and respected. Authentic communication ensures that every voice is acknowledged and heard, regardless of cultural or background differences. Recognizing individual uniqueness builds trust among team members and encourages them to contribute their insights without hesitation. When employees feel their perspectives are genuinely valued, they are more likely to actively collaborate, share innovative ideas, and work collectively to find solutions to challenges.

Fundamentally, authenticity in communication breaks down barriers that might otherwise hinder effective collaboration. It bridges cultural gaps, fosters a sense of belonging, and creates an atmosphere where employees feel comfortable expressing their thoughts and opinions. This level of trust and respect leads to more vital teamwork and synergy as diverse perspectives create comprehensive and well-rounded solutions.

Culturally diverse organizations build a foundation for productive collaboration by nurturing authentic communication and valuing all individuals' contributions. This collaboration improves overall performance and enriches the organization's culture by promoting inclusivity and demonstrating that each individual's voice matters.

Driving Organizational Success: Embracing authenticity within culturally diverse organizations is not just a matter of fostering a welcoming atmosphere; it is a strategic imperative for driving overall organizational success. The profound impact of authenticity reaches deep into the core of the organization, influencing various facets that contribute to its performance and reputation.

At the heart of this impact is the direct effect on employees. When organizations prioritize authenticity, it sends a clear message that individuality and diverse perspectives are not only accepted but celebrated. This acknowledgment fosters a sense of belonging and purpose among employees, enhancing their motivation, commitment, and loyalty to the organization. Employees who feel their authentic selves are valued are more likely to invest their energy and dedication into their roles, leading to increased job satisfaction and a stronger work ethic.

Beyond the internal dynamics, authenticity significantly shapes the external image of an organization. A culture of authenticity not only attracts top talent but retains it as well. In today's competitive job market, job seekers are drawn to organizations that prioritize inclusivity and respect for diverse backgrounds. Authenticity serves as a magnet for skilled professionals who want to be part of an environment where their contributions are genuinely valued, regardless of their cultural or identity-based differences.

Innovation is another domain significantly impacted by authenticity. When individuals are free to express themselves authentically, it paves the way for innovative thinking. Diverse perspectives bring fresh insights and novel solutions to the table, driving creativity and problem-solving. Embracing authenticity in a culturally diverse setting enables organizations to tap into this wealth of creativity, leading to the development of more inventive products, services, and strategies.

Moreover, authenticity plays a pivotal role in building strong relationships with diverse customer bases. Consumers are increasingly drawn to organizations that align with their values, including those related to diversity and inclusion. An authentic commitment to these values resonates with customers, creating a sense of trust and connection. This connection can translate into customer loyalty and positive word-of-mouth, boosting the organization's reputation and market presence.

Intrinsically, embracing authenticity isn't just a feel-good measure; it's a strategic driver of organizational success. By fostering an environment where authenticity is valued and encouraged, organizations harness the power of their culturally diverse workforce. This leads to heightened competitiveness, adaptability, and resilience in an ever-evolving business landscape. The ripple effects of authenticity extend to employee engagement, innovation, customer relationships, and the organization's overall ability to thrive in a diverse and dynamic world.

Showcasing Successful Corporate Minority Leaders

Embracing cultural diversity and promoting authentic leadership is paramount for organizations across various sectors seeking to thrive in today's interconnected world. Recognizing the power of culturally authentic identities in leadership roles, successful organizations have made significant strides in creating environments where minority leaders can embrace and utilize their unique perspectives and experiences. From the corporate sector to nonprofits, higher education institutions, and government entities, these organizations have demonstrated a commitment to diversity, equity, and inclusion by fostering culturally diverse environments that empower minority leaders to lead authentically. Let's explore real examples of organizations in each sector that have successfully embraced cultural authenticity and created inclusive spaces for minority leaders to flourish and make a meaningful impact.

Corporate Sector: One example of a successful organization in the corporate sector that has created a culturally diverse environment where minority leaders can embrace and utilize their culturally authentic identity is Microsoft. Microsoft has made significant strides in promoting diversity and inclusion throughout the company, recognizing the importance of embracing cultural authenticity in leadership.

Through initiatives such as its Employee Resource Groups (ERGs) and diversity training programs, Microsoft actively fosters an inclusive culture where employees can bring their whole selves to work. They provide platforms for underrepresented employees, including minority leaders, to connect, share experiences, and contribute to organizational decision-making processes. Microsoft's commitment to cultural authenticity and diversity has led to a more inclusive workplace and resulted in innovative solutions and increased productivity, positioning the company as a leader in the technology industry.

Nonprofit Sector: An example of a successful nonprofit organization supporting culturally authentic leadership is the Ford Foundation. The Ford Foundation has a long-standing commitment to diversity, equity, and inclusion and recognizes the importance of embracing culturally authentic leadership to address systemic issues and drive social change. The foundation actively seeks diverse perspectives and experiences among its staff and administration, ensuring that minority leaders can bring their unique cultural backgrounds and identities to their roles. By valuing and supporting culturally authentic leadership, the Ford Foundation empowers minority leaders to make a meaningful impact in addressing social and economic inequalities worldwide. Their approach fosters collaboration, drives innovation, and strengthens the foundation's ability to create positive and lasting social change.

Higher Education: In the higher education sector, the University of California, Los Angeles (UCLA) is a notable example of an institution promoting culturally authentic leadership. UCLA is firmly committed to diversity and inclusion, recognizing that embracing cultural authenticity is vital for creating a supportive environment for students and faculty. The university actively recruits and supports minority leaders who bring unique cultural perspectives to academic leadership roles. Through programs like the Faculty Diversity Initiative, UCLA provides resources, mentorship, and opportunities for career advancement, empowering minority leaders to excel in their academic and administrative roles. By embracing and valuing culturally authentic leadership, UCLA enhances the educational experience for all students and promotes an inclusive campus climate that celebrates diversity.

Government: The Canadian government exemplifies successful efforts to create a culturally diverse environment that allows minority leaders to embrace and utilize their culturally authentic identity. The government of Canada has been proactive in implementing policies and initiatives to promote diversity and inclusion in leadership roles. Through programs like the Federal Internship for Newcomers (FIN) and the Visible Minority Newcomer Women Pilot, the government supports the professional development and advancement of minority leaders from diverse cultural backgrounds. These initiatives aim to break down barriers, increase representation, and ensure that minority leaders can bring their authentic perspectives to the decision-making processes of the government. By embracing and leveraging culturally authentic leadership, the Canadian government creates a more equitable and inclusive society where diverse voices are heard and valued.

These examples showcase successful organizations in different sectors prioritizing and creating culturally diverse environments where minority leaders can embrace and utilize their culturally authentic identities. Through their commitment to diversity, equity, and inclusion, these organizations have enhanced their internal cultures, fostered innovation, driven social change, and positively impacted their respective sectors.

Authentic leadership's core lies in the recognition and embrace of personal identity. When organizations and leaders honor their authentic selves, they create a space for others to do the same, fostering a culture of inclusivity and empowerment. This section explored the importance of self-awareness and reflection in understanding one's identity and how it shapes leadership styles, values, and decision-making. We examined the significance of cultural heritage, lived experiences, and the intersections of identities in shaping a leader's unique perspective. By embracing personal identity, leaders and their respective organizations can bring their whole selves to their roles, inspiring trust, fostering meaningful connections, and unleashing their true potential as catalysts for change. Through this exploration, we uncover the transformative power of authenticity and identity in driving inclusive and impactful leadership.

Questions for Leadership Discussion

1. How can embracing cultural authenticity contribute to fostering a sense of belonging and psychological safety within my/our organization?

2. In what ways does embracing authenticity in culturally diverse organizations enhance communication and collaboration among team members?

3. How can my/our organization address systemic inequities and biases by recognizing and valuing the intersectionality of identity in leadership?

4. What strategies can my/our organization employ to empower underrepresented leaders and create inclusive leadership development programs that address the specific needs of individuals with intersecting identities?

5. What are the long-term benefits of embracing authenticity in a culturally diverse organization, and how does it contribute to overall organizational success, innovation, and employee engagement?

CHAPTER FOUR

The Wisdom of Experience: Leveraging Age in Leadership

"

By recognizing and leveraging the wisdom gained through a lifetime of experiences, organizations can foster inclusive leadership environments that harness the power of diverse perspectives, ultimately leading to greater success and sustainable outcomes.

There is a tendency to emphasize youth and innovation as the primary drivers of successful leadership. The prevailing narrative often centers around the notion that fresh ideas, cutting-edge technologies, and a forward-thinking mindset are the key to organizational success. While these elements hold value, it is essential to recognize that age brings a wealth of wisdom, experience, and invaluable insights that can significantly contribute to effective leadership. Leaders who have weathered the storms of time possess a deep reservoir of knowledge from overcoming challenges, navigating complex situations, and making tough decisions. This chapter aims to challenge the prevailing stereotypes and shed light on the untapped potential of older leaders. By understanding and leveraging the wisdom gained through a lifetime of experiences, organizations can foster inclusive leadership environments that harness the power of diverse perspectives, ultimately leading to tremendous success and sustainable outcomes.

As leaders mature and accumulate experience, they develop a nuanced understanding of their industry, organization, and the intricacies of human behavior. This depth of knowledge enables them to make well-informed judgments, anticipate potential pitfalls, and offer practical solutions based on proven methods. With age, leaders often develop a comprehensive perspective encompassing the big picture and the subtle nuances of organizational dynamics. This ability to see beyond immediate challenges and consider long-term implications can lead to more strategic decision-making and the avoidance of costly mistakes.

Moreover, older leaders often possess a heightened emotional intelligence honed through years of interacting with diverse individuals and managing complex relationships. This emotional intelligence allows them to effectively navigate interpersonal dynamics, resolve conflicts, and foster collaboration. Drawing from their past experiences, they have honed their communication skills, empathy, and ability to inspire and motivate teams. Their well-developed emotional intelligence can create an inclusive and supportive work environment where all team members feel valued, respected, and empowered to contribute their best.

However, it is crucial to acknowledge that age diversity in leadership also presents challenges. Stereotypes and biases based on age can undermine the contributions and potential of older leaders. Ageism, the discrimination or unfair treatment of individuals based on age, can hinder opportunities for more senior leaders to access top positions or participate in innovative projects. Overcoming these biases and creating a culture that values and appreciates the unique strengths of older leaders is a vital step toward harnessing the full potential of age diversity in leadership.

Throughout this chapter, we will delve into the unique strengths that come with age in leadership positions, examine the challenges older leaders face, and explore strategies to leverage the wisdom of experience for organizational success. By embracing age diversity and recognizing the immense value of more senior leaders, organizations can create a more balanced and inclusive leadership landscape that celebrates the diverse range of perspectives, skills, and experiences that contribute to transformative leadership and sustainable growth.

The Unique Strengths and Challenges of Age Diversity

Strength: Wisdom and Experience: Older leaders possess a remarkable depth of wisdom and experience acquired through years of navigating the complexities of their careers. This wisdom stems from a combination of accumulated knowledge, lessons learned from successes and failures, and a refined understanding of the intricacies of their field. Their extensive knowledge base is a valuable resource for decision-making, as they draw upon a vast repertoire of past experiences to inform their choices. Having encountered various challenges and opportunities throughout their careers, they can offer practical insights beyond textbook theories, enabling them to anticipate potential obstacles and devise effective strategies to overcome them.

Furthermore, the wisdom and experience of older leaders make them well-suited to mentor and guide younger professionals. Their deep understanding of industry trends, historical contexts, and organizational dynamics allows them to provide invaluable guidance and support to the next generation of leaders. By sharing their knowledge and lessons learned, they help to accelerate the growth and development of younger professionals, empowering them to navigate the complexities of their chosen field. Through mentoring relationships, older leaders can pass down their accumulated wisdom and provide practical advice that can shape the future leaders of organizations. Their mentorship serves as a valuable source of guidance, fostering the growth and success of emerging talent.

The strength of wisdom and experience in older leaders lies in their extensive knowledge, practical insights, and ability to mentor others. Their deep understanding of industry trends, historical contexts, and organizational dynamics empowers them to make informed decisions and guide the next generation. By leveraging their accumulated wisdom and experience, organizations can tap into a valuable resource that contributes to effective leadership, informed decision-making, and the overall success and growth of the organization.

Challenge: Adapting to Technological Advancements: One of the challenges that older leaders may encounter is keeping pace with rapidly evolving technologies and digital transformation. As technology advances at an unprecedented rate, older leaders may find it challenging to adapt to new technologies and effectively leverage digital tools in their leadership roles. The rapid changes in the technology landscape can lead to a technological gap between older and younger leaders, as the latter may have grown up with digital technologies and are more familiar with their applications. This technological gap can challenge more senior leaders to understand and harness the full potential of emerging technologies, which are increasingly becoming integral to business operations and strategies.

Acquiring new technical skills and adapting to digital platforms may require additional support and training for older leaders. The learning curve associated with mastering new technologies and digital tools can be steep, especially for those not immersed in the digital landscape throughout their careers. To overcome this challenge, organizations must recognize the importance of providing targeted opportunities for upskilling and reskilling for older leaders. These opportunities may involve offering specialized training programs, workshops, or mentoring support tailored to their specific technological needs. By investing in their development, organizations can bridge the technological gap and equip older leaders with the skills and knowledge necessary to effectively navigate the digital landscape and leverage technology to drive innovation and organizational success.

The challenge of adapting to technological advancements pertains to the need for older leaders to keep pace with rapidly evolving technologies and digital transformation. Acquiring new technical skills and adapting to digital platforms may require additional support and training. Organizations have a crucial role in addressing this challenge by providing targeted opportunities for upskilling and reskilling, ensuring that older leaders can navigate the digital landscape and leverage technology to drive organizational success. By proactively bridging the technological gap, organizations can harness older leaders' valuable experience and wisdom while enabling them to thrive in a technology-driven world.

Strength: Long-Term Perspective: One of the strengths that older leaders bring to the table is their long-term perspective, shaped by their extensive experiences and historical context. Having spent significant time in their respective industries or organizations, they have witnessed and navigated various economic cycles, market fluctuations, and industry shifts. This breadth of experience allows them to anticipate trends and changes that may impact the organization in the long run. By drawing upon their historical knowledge, older leaders can identify patterns and make informed predictions about future developments, enabling them to stay ahead of the curve and proactively position the organization for success.

Furthermore, the long-term perspective of older leaders empowers them to identify potential risks and opportunities that may arise over time. Their seasoned judgment enables them to evaluate different courses of action, considering immediate benefits and long-term implications. By weighing short-term gains against sustainable outcomes, they can make strategic decisions that align with the organization's vision and goals. This ability to balance immediate needs and long-term sustainability contributes to organizational resilience. Older leaders can guide the organization through changing landscapes while keeping sight of the bigger picture, ensuring that their decisions align with its core values and long-term aspirations.

The strength of a long-term perspective in older leaders stems from their experiences and historical context. By leveraging their extensive knowledge and insights, they can anticipate trends, identify risks, and make strategic decisions that align with the organization's vision. Their ability to balance immediate goals with long-term sustainability contributes to the organization's resilience and positions it for long-term success in an ever-changing business environment.

Challenge: Overcoming Ageism and Stereotypes: One of the significant challenges that older leaders may face is overcoming ageism, biases, and stereotypes that can hinder the recognition of their valuable contributions. Ageism refers to the discrimination or unfair treatment of individuals based on their age, and it can manifest in various forms within organizational settings. Biases and stereotypes based on age can lead to negative perceptions and preconceived notions about older leaders, limiting their opportunities for advancement, development, and involvement in strategic initiatives. This bias can create barriers that prevent organizations from fully utilizing the expertise, experience, and wisdom that older leaders bring.

Negative perceptions that older leaders are resistant to change or less innovative can further undermine their potential impact and contribution. Such stereotypes overlook the adaptive capabilities, flexibility, and capacity for innovation that older leaders possess. By assuming that older leaders are less open to change or cannot generate fresh ideas, organizations may miss out on unique perspectives and insights from years of experience and accumulated wisdom. Overcoming these biases and stereotypes is crucial to unlocking the total value of age diversity in leadership and enabling organizations to benefit from the rich knowledge and diverse perspectives that older leaders bring.

Challenging these biases and promoting inclusive leadership practices is essential for organizations to foster an environment where all stakeholders can realize the total value of age diversity. It requires organizations to proactively address ageism and stereotypes by promoting awareness, education, and a culture of inclusivity. Inclusive leadership can be achieved through training programs that promote diversity and inclusion, creating mentorship opportunities that bridge generational gaps, and implementing policies that foster intergenerational collaboration. By recognizing and valuing the contributions of older leaders, organizations can create an environment that embraces diversity in all its forms and leverages the unique strengths and perspectives that come with age diversity. Ultimately, embracing age diversity allows organizations to tap into a broader range of talent and experiences, leading to enhanced innovation, better decision-making, and improved organizational performance.

Strength: Emotional Intelligence and Interpersonal Skills: One of the strengths that older leaders bring to the table is their well-developed emotional intelligence and interpersonal skills, which face many challenges over years of experience. Older leaders have had ample time to refine their communication abilities through their extensive professional journey. They possess the capacity to express themselves clearly and effectively, whether in one-on-one interactions, group settings or when addressing larger audiences. Their refined communication skills allow them to precisely articulate their thoughts, ideas, and vision, ensuring that their messages are understood and resonate with their teams.

In addition to solid communication abilities, older leaders often display a heightened sense of empathy. They have had numerous opportunities to engage with diverse individuals, work through conflicts, and understand the perspectives of others. This empathy enables them to relate to their team members on a deeper level, considering their needs, concerns, and motivations. By demonstrating empathy, older leaders create a supportive and inclusive work environment where individuals feel valued, heard, and understood. Empathy fosters trust, cooperation, and collaboration among team members, enhancing productivity and a positive team dynamic.

Furthermore, the adeptness of older leaders in managing diverse teams and resolving conflicts contributes to a positive work environment. They have encountered various team dynamics and navigated challenging situations throughout their careers.

This experience equips them with a range of conflict-resolution strategies, negotiation techniques, and problem-solving skills. Older leaders understand the importance of recognizing and appreciating team members' diverse perspectives and strengths. They create an inclusive space where everyone feels valued, encouraged to contribute their unique insights, and supported in their professional growth. By effectively managing diverse teams, older leaders cultivate an environment that celebrates collaboration, innovation, and mutual respect, improving morale, engagement, and overall team performance.

Older leaders' emotional intelligence and interpersonal skills are strengthened by their refined communication abilities, heightened empathy, and adeptness in managing diverse teams. Their well-developed emotional intelligence enables them to establish strong relationships, create a positive work environment, and effectively address conflicts when they arise. By leveraging these strengths, older leaders foster an inclusive and supportive culture where individuals can thrive, collaborate, and achieve their full potential.

Strength: Mentoring and Knowledge: One of the critical strengths of older leaders is their ability to serve as mentors, passing on their knowledge, skills, and experiences to the next generation of leaders. With their accumulated wealth of expertise throughout their careers, older leaders are well-positioned to guide and support younger employees in their professional growth. By sharing their insights, lessons learned, and industry-specific knowledge, they can help aspiring leaders navigate the challenges and complexities of their chosen field. Through their mentorship, older leaders offer valuable perspectives, practical advice, and guidance that can accelerate the development and success of younger professionals.

The guidance and support older leaders provide in mentoring relationships can profoundly impact the professional growth of younger employees. Drawing on their own experiences, older leaders can offer a unique perspective beyond formal education or training programs. They provide guidance on career paths, offer insights into decision-making, and share wisdom gained from navigating various work-related situations. The mentorship of older leaders instills confidence in young professionals, enabling them to make informed choices, overcome obstacles, and capitalize on opportunities. The guidance and support provided by older leaders can fast-track the professional growth of younger employees, empowering them to reach their full potential and make a meaningful impact in their careers.

Moreover, mentoring programs facilitated by older leaders contribute to a culture of continuous learning and development within organizations. By formalizing mentorship relationships and providing structured opportunities for knowledge transfer, organizations create an environment that promotes ongoing learning and growth. These programs allow younger employees to access the wealth of expertise and experience older leaders possess, fostering a spirit of collaboration and knowledge-sharing. The establishment of mentoring programs facilitated by older leaders not only enhances the professional development of younger employees but also promotes the preservation and transfer of organizational knowledge, values, and best practices. It creates a dynamic learning ecosystem where wisdom is passed down from generation to generation, cultivating a culture of continuous improvement and ensuring the organization remains adaptable and resilient in a rapidly changing world.

In summary, the strength of mentoring and knowledge transfer lies in older leaders' ability to serve as mentors, guiding and supporting the next generation of leaders. Their mentorship can accelerate the professional growth of younger employees by providing insights, advice, and support based on their own experiences. Additionally, mentoring programs facilitated by older leaders foster a culture of continuous learning and development within organizations, creating a knowledge-sharing environment that benefits both mentors and mentees. By leveraging the strengths of mentoring and knowledge transfer, organizations can cultivate a talented and empowered workforce equipped to drive innovation, adapt to change, and achieve sustainable success.

Navigating these strengths and challenges requires organizations to create an inclusive environment that values age diversity, promotes intergenerational collaboration, and fosters ongoing learning opportunities. By leveraging the unique strengths of older leaders and addressing the challenges they may face, organizations can harness the full potential of age diversity, driving innovation and sustainable success.

Recognizing the Valuable Roles of Experienced Leaders

In maximizing the potential and effectiveness of an organization, it is essential to recognize the valuable roles of experienced leaders. These leaders, with their years of knowledge, wisdom, and expertise, bring a unique set of skills and perspectives that can significantly contribute to the success and growth of the organization. By acknowledging and harnessing the valuable contributions of experienced leaders, organizations can tap into a wealth of insights, foster mentorship, knowledge transfer, promote stability, and leverage institutional memory. In the following section, we will delve into the key reasons why recognizing the valuable roles of experienced leaders is crucial and explore the benefits it brings to organizations regarding wisdom and expertise, mentorship and knowledge transfer, and stability and continuity.

Institutional Memory and Historical Context: Experienced leaders have a unique advantage in deeply understanding the organization's history, culture, and legacy. They have witnessed and actively participated in the organization's evolution. This invaluable institutional memory provides a critical context for decision-making and strategic planning. By recognizing the valuable roles of experienced leaders, organizations can tap into this rich knowledge base and leverage it to inform present and future actions.

The insights and historical context offered by experienced leaders help shape decision-making processes by providing a broader perspective. Their understanding of past successes, failures, and lessons learned allows them to draw upon real-life experiences to guide current initiatives. By learning from the organization's history, they can identify patterns, anticipate challenges, and capitalize on opportunities. This knowledge helps avoid repeated mistakes and build upon past achievements, resulting in more informed and effective leadership.

Furthermore, experienced leaders' institutional memory is instrumental in preserving the organization's culture and values. They understand the norms, traditions, and shared beliefs that define the organization's identity. By recognizing the valuable roles of experienced leaders, organizations ensure that this institutional memory is preserved and remembered. Leveraging their insights into the organization's cultural fabric allows for a more holistic understanding of how decisions impact various stakeholders and align with its core principles. This preservation of historical context and cultural awareness contributes to maintaining the organization's identity, fostering a sense of continuity, and guiding strategic planning that respects and honors the organization's heritage.

recognizing the valuable roles of experienced leaders preservation of institutional memory and historical context enables organizations to tap into their deep understanding of the organization's history, culture, and legacy. By leveraging their insights, organizations can make more informed decisions, avoid repeated mistakes, and build upon past achievements. Preserving institutional memory fosters continuity and helps shape strategic planning that aligns with the organization's values and long-term goals. Ultimately, this recognition contributes to effective leadership and the organization's sustained success.

Relationship Building and Networks: Experienced leaders have had the opportunity to cultivate extensive networks of relationships within their industries and sectors. Throughout their careers, they have interacted with various individuals, including colleagues, industry peers, clients, suppliers, and experts in their field. Recognizing the valuable roles of experienced leaders allows organizations to tap into these networks and leverage them for various purposes.

The relationships experienced leaders have built over time provide organizations with valuable access to business opportunities, partnerships, and collaborations. Through their network of connections, they can identify potential clients, establish strategic alliances, and explore new markets. Their relationships with key stakeholders and industry experts can open doors to valuable resources, knowledge, and support that benefit the organization. These connections can provide insights into industry trends, emerging technologies, and market dynamics, helping the organization stay competitive and adapt to changing circumstances.

Moreover, the valuable connections of experienced leaders can contribute to the organization's growth, reputation, and strategic positioning within markets and industries. Their established relationships with clients and stakeholders can foster trust, loyalty, and long-term partnerships. Strong relationships can lead to repeat business, positive word-of-mouth referrals, and enhanced brand recognition. The network of connections also enables organizations to tap into diverse perspectives and expertise, accessing a more comprehensive range of skills and knowledge that can drive innovation and problem-solving.

Acknowledging the valuable roles of experienced leaders allows organizations to leverage the extensive networks of relationships they have built. These networks provide access to business opportunities, partnerships, and collaborations, facilitating growth and strategic positioning. The connections established by experienced leaders contribute to the organization's reputation, access to resources, and ability to tap into diverse expertise. By recognizing and harnessing these valuable relationships, organizations can enhance their competitive advantage and foster mutually beneficial collaborations that drive success.

Stability and Continuity: Recognizing the valuable roles of experienced leaders is essential in promoting peace and continuity within the organization. Experienced leaders' familiarity with the organization's operations, systems, and processes allows them to serve as stabilizing forces during times of change or transition. Their deep understanding of how things work and their ability to navigate complex organizational dynamics contribute to maintaining stability, even in the face of uncertainty.

Experienced leaders bring a sense of continuity to the organization by ensuring that institutional knowledge is preserved and carried forward. They possess a historical context and awareness of past decisions, strategies, and outcomes. This knowledge allows them to make informed decisions and guide the organization in a manner that builds upon previous successes and avoids repeating past mistakes. By leveraging their experience and understanding of the organization's history, experienced leaders provide a sense of direction and purpose, ensuring that the organization remains on track and aligned with its long-term goals.

The stability and continuity-oriented leadership of experienced leaders also provides reassurance to employees, stakeholders, and investors. Their presence and steady guidance during times of change or uncertainty instill confidence and trust. Employees feel supported and are more likely to remain engaged and productive when they have leaders who can offer stability and a sense of direction. Stakeholders and investors also value the presence of experienced leaders who can effectively manage challenges and navigate disruptions, contributing to the organization's resilience and longevity.

Identifying the valuable roles of experienced leaders promotes stability and continuity within the organization. Their familiarity with operations, systems, and processes allows them to maintain stability during times of change. Their ability to preserve and carry forward institutional knowledge ensures that essential functions can continue seamlessly. The stability and continuity-oriented leadership of experienced leaders provides reassurance to employees, stakeholders, and investors, fostering organizational resilience and contributing to long-term success.

Successful Minority Leaders Defying Age-Related Adversity

Ursula Burns' leadership journey at Xerox Corporation is a remarkable example of a successful corporate minority leader defying age-related biases and making a significant impact. When she became the CEO in 2009, Burns was in her 50s, which was considered relatively older in the corporate world. However, she proved that age should not hinder success, breaking barriers as the first African American woman to lead a Fortune 500 company.

During her tenure as CEO, Burns focused on transforming Xerox into a service-led technology company. She recognized the need to adapt to a changing industry landscape and initiated strategic moves to position the company for success. Burns led Xerox through a series of acquisitions, expanding its digital offerings and diversifying its portfolio. Her vision and strategic decisions enabled Xerox to stay competitive and drive significant growth in new markets.

Burns' leadership at Xerox led to the company's success and made her a role model for aspiring corporate leaders. Her remarkable achievements and ability to navigate through challenges demonstrated that age should not be a limiting factor in achieving one's goals. Burns shattered glass ceilings, inspiring others and showcasing the value experienced leaders bring to organizations regardless of age.

Ursula Burns' story is a testament to the power of resilience, vision, and perseverance in the face of age-related biases. She exemplifies how experienced leaders can drive transformative change and create a lasting impact, challenging societal norms and paving the way for future generations of diverse corporate leaders.

Warren Buffett is another real-life example of a successful leader who, for this section, is considered a member of the aging minority demographic. As one of the world's most renowned investors and the Chairman and CEO of Berkshire Hathaway Inc., Buffett has achieved remarkable success despite his older age. Buffett, often referred to as the "Oracle of Omaha," has built Berkshire Hathaway into a multinational conglomerate with a diverse portfolio of businesses.

Buffett's investment strategies and long-term perspective have been instrumental in his success. Despite being in his 80s, Buffett continues to lead Berkshire Hathaway and make significant investment decisions. His wisdom, experience, and ability to identify long-term value have earned him a reputation as one of the most successful investors in history. Buffett's continued leadership and ability to adapt to changing market dynamics have solidified his position as a respected corporate leader, breaking stereotypes about older leaders' ability to thrive and excel in business.

Both Burns and Buffett are prime examples of successful corporate minority leaders who have defied age-related biases and made a significant impact. Their stories emphasize the importance of recognizing the valuable roles of experienced leaders, regardless of age, and leveraging their wisdom, experience, and unique perspectives for organizational success. These leaders exemplify the immense value seasoned leaders bring to organizations and industries, challenging societal norms and inspiring future generations of diverse corporate leaders.

Questions for Leadership Discussion

1. How does the prevailing emphasis on youth and innovation in leadership impact the recognition of the wisdom and experience that older leaders bring to the table?

2. What strategies can organizations implement to bridge the technological gap between older and younger leaders and ensure that older leaders can effectively leverage emerging technologies?

3. How can organizations overcome ageism and stereotypes to fully harness the emotional intelligence and interpersonal skills of older leaders and create inclusive leadership environments?

Chapter Five

Breaking Barriers: Gender Equality in Organizational Leadership

"

The pursuit of gender equality in leadership is not only a matter of fairness and social justice but also a strategic imperative for organizations and societies at large.

The pursuit of gender equality in leadership is not only a matter of fairness and social justice but also a strategic imperative for organizations and societies at large. Despite significant progress in recent years, women face numerous barriers and biases that hinder their advancement into leadership roles. Breaking these barriers and achieving true gender equality in leadership is essential for creating inclusive workplaces and unlocking the full potential of diverse perspectives and talents. This chapter explores the challenges women encounter in their journey to leadership, examines the underlying factors contributing to gender disparities, and highlights strategies and initiatives to break the glass ceiling and foster gender equality in leadership positions. By understanding the complexities of this issue and taking action, we can create more equitable and thriving leadership landscapes that benefit individuals and organizations and limit gender biases.

Unpacking the Gender Dynamics in Leadership Roles

Gender dynamics play a significant role in shaping the landscape of leadership positions, with long-standing biases and stereotypes often disadvantaging women. Historically, men have predominantly occupied leadership roles, perpetuating a system that favors masculine traits and norms. These gender dynamics create challenges for women aspiring to reach top leadership positions as they navigate societal expectations, implicit biases, and limited representation. Understanding the gender dynamics at play is crucial for addressing the barriers that hinder women's progression and fostering a more inclusive and diverse leadership landscape.

One prominent aspect of gender dynamics in leadership is the prevalence of stereotypes and biases against women. Deeply ingrained societal beliefs often associate leadership qualities with assertiveness, confidence, and decisiveness, traits traditionally associated with masculinity. As a result, women may face scrutiny and skepticism when exhibiting these qualities, often labeled as "too aggressive" or "bossy." These stereotypes limit the opportunities available to women and create a double standard in evaluating their leadership potential. Unpacking and challenging these biases is essential for creating a level playing field and empowering women to thrive in leadership roles.

Another critical aspect of gender dynamics in leadership is the impact of structural and systemic barriers. Women often face obstacles rooted in organizational structures, policies, and cultural norms that impede their advancement. For example, the lack of flexible work arrangements, limited access to mentoring and sponsorship opportunities, and biased promotion processes can restrict women's progress and contribute to gender disparities in leadership. Recognizing and addressing these structural barriers is vital for dismantling the systemic inequalities that prevent women from reaching their full leadership potential.

The intersectionality of gender dynamics adds another layer of complexity to women's experiences in leadership. Women from marginalized and underrepresented groups face unique challenges due to the combined effects of gender bias and other forms of discrimination, such as racism or ableism. The intersectional lens allows us to understand how various identities intersect and shape women's opportunities, experiences, and barriers in leadership. By recognizing and addressing these intersecting dynamics, organizations can create more inclusive environments that embrace and uplift women from diverse backgrounds.

Power imbalances and implicit biases also contribute to gender dynamics in leadership. The underrepresentation of women in positions of power perpetuates a cycle where decision-making and influence remain concentrated in the hands of a few. This lack of diversity limits the perspectives and insights brought to the table and perpetuates the notion that men are more competent or suitable for leadership roles. Addressing these power imbalances requires deliberate efforts to increase women's representation in leadership positions, challenge existing norms, and promote inclusive decision-making processes.

While the challenges are evident, it is essential to recognize that gender dynamics in leadership roles are not fixed or insurmountable. Progress has advanced in recent years, with organizations and societies recognizing the value of gender diversity and taking steps to promote equal opportunities. Initiatives such as mentorship programs, diversity and inclusion training, and gender-neutral policies have shown promise in dismantling gender biases and creating more inclusive leadership cultures. By continuing to unpack and address gender dynamics, organizations can foster environments where women can thrive, contribute their unique talents, and lead with authenticity, ultimately advancing gender equality in leadership.

Gender dynamics in leadership roles also extend to the perception and evaluation of women's leadership styles. Research has shown that women often face a "double bind," where the expectation is to display traditionally feminine traits, such as empathy, nurturing, assertiveness, and authority. Straying too far in either direction can result in negative evaluations and perceptions. This bias can limit the range of leadership styles that women feel comfortable employing and can lead to a narrowing of opportunities for advancement. Recognizing and valuing diverse leadership styles, irrespective of gender, is crucial for creating a more inclusive leadership landscape.

The lack of gender diversity in leadership can also perpetuate stereotypes and reinforce the notion that women are not suited for leadership roles. Limited representation of women in top positions creates a vicious cycle where the absence of role models and mentors hinders the progress of aspiring female leaders. Breaking through this cycle requires intentional efforts to identify and address the underlying biases contributing to women's underrepresentation in leadership roles. Organizations can play a vital role by implementing policies and practices that actively promote and support the advancement of women, fostering an environment where women can see themselves in leadership positions.

The impact of gender dynamics in leadership extends beyond individual experiences to organizational culture and performance. Research consistently demonstrates that gender-diverse leadership teams are associated with better financial performance, enhanced decision-making, and increased innovation. By leveraging the diverse perspectives and skills that women bring to the table, organizations can benefit from a broader range of insights and a more comprehensive understanding of their stakeholders. Embracing gender diversity in leadership is a matter of equality, fairness, and a strategic advantage that drives organizational success.

It is essential to acknowledge that gender dynamics in leadership roles can also affect men. Expectations to conform to traditional masculine leadership norms, limiting their ability to express vulnerability, empathy, or collaborative approaches, are also experienced by men within organizations. By unpacking and challenging gender norms and expectations for men and women, organizations can create environments that support diverse leadership styles and enable all individuals to lead authentically and effectively.

Addressing gender dynamics in leadership requires a comprehensive and intersectional approach that considers the unique experiences and challenges different groups of women face. Recognizing that gender is not a homogenous category but intersects with race, ethnicity, age, ability, and other identities is essential for designing effective strategies and interventions. Organizations must prioritize inclusivity and equity by fostering cultures that value diversity, providing equal opportunities for growth and development, and proactively challenging biases and stereotypes. By doing so, organizations can not only advance gender equality in leadership but also create more equitable and just societies.

Addressing Gender Biases and Stereotypes in Leadership

Gender biases and stereotypes are prevalent in male-dominated and female-dominated organizational leadership structures. In male-dominated fields, such as technology or finance, women often face preconceived notions that they are less competent or suited for leadership roles. Stereotypes that associate women with nurturing and caretaking functions can undermine their credibility and make it challenging for them to gain recognition and authority. Similarly, men who aspire to leadership positions in traditionally female-dominated industries, such as nursing or education, may encounter biases that question their abilities or suggest they are not a good fit for those roles.

Challenging these biases and creating more inclusive environments is crucial for breaking down barriers and enabling individuals to excel based on their skills and qualifications rather than gender stereotypes.

In male-dominated leadership structures, gender biases can manifest as the "glass ceiling" phenomenon, where women face invisible barriers that hinder their advancement to top leadership positions. Stereotypes that portray women as lacking in assertiveness or executive presence can impede their access to promotions and opportunities for leadership development. Moreover, the scarcity of female role models and mentors in these industries can exacerbate these biases and further limit women's progression. Organizations must actively work to dismantle these biases, promote gender diversity at all levels of leadership, and create a supportive and inclusive culture that values the contributions of women.

In contrast, female-dominated leadership structures can also be subject to gender biases and stereotypes. Consider an example in primary education, which is often female dominated. In an industry where women account for more than fifty percent of all principals, men who pursue careers as primary school teachers with aspirations to advance into leadership might also encounter "glass ceiling" biases. Despite their qualifications and dedication, male teachers may struggle to move into leadership roles such as head teachers or principals, thus highlighting the importance of recognizing biases that can hinder career progression for both genders in different industries. It also underscores the need to create environments that value skills and qualifications over gender stereotypes, ultimately fostering inclusive workplaces that benefit everyone's growth and development. We must continue to challenge the notion that specific industries or professions are inherently better suited for individuals of one particular gender and create opportunities for all individuals to thrive and contribute their unique talents and perspectives.

Addressing gender biases and stereotypes in male-dominated and female-dominated leadership structures necessitates dismantling societal norms and expectations that prescribe specific gender roles and capabilities. Individuals, organizations, and society must challenge ingrained biases, question assumptions, and cultivate a culture of inclusivity. Men and women must work together to break down barriers, promote equality, and create opportunities for leadership success based on merit rather than gender stereotypes. By doing so, organizations can foster diverse and dynamic leadership teams that drive innovation, enhance decision-making, and create a more enjoyable and cohesive workplace experience for all stakeholders.

Achieving gender equality in male-dominated and female-dominated leadership structures requires a multifaceted approach encompassing education, awareness, and policy changes. Engaging in open dialogues, providing training on unconscious bias, and creating mentoring programs that empower individuals to challenge stereotypes and biases within their organizations is crucial. By fostering an environment that values diversity and inclusivity, organizations can dismantle gender biases and stereotypes, creating opportunities for all individuals to thrive and contribute their unique talents, regardless of the dominant gender dynamics in their respective industries.

The Progress and Roadblocks in Achieving Gender Parity

Significant progress has been evident in recent years toward achieving gender parity within organizations, but roadblocks still hinder the realization of true equality. One notable area of improvement is the increasing representation of women in leadership positions. Many organizations have implemented diversity and inclusion initiatives, such as gender quotas, mentorship programs, and unconscious bias training, to promote gender parity actively. These efforts have resulted in more women breaking through the glass ceiling and assuming influential roles within their organizations. However, despite these advances, gender parity remains a work in progress, and numerous roadblocks persist.

One of the primary roadblocks to achieving gender parity is the persistence of unconscious biases and gender stereotypes. These biases can shape perceptions, decision-making processes, and opportunities within organizations, creating barriers for women to access leadership roles and reach their full potential. Stereotypes that associate leadership qualities with masculine traits can perpetuate the notion that women are less suited for senior positions. Addressing these biases requires continuous education and awareness-raising efforts to challenge and dismantle gender stereotypes, promoting a more inclusive and equitable culture that values diverse leadership styles and contributions.

Another significant roadblock to gender parity is the lack of work-life balance and support systems for women. Traditional gender roles and societal expectations often place a disproportionate burden on women to fulfill caregiving and household responsibilities, limiting their ability to commit to their careers and pursue leadership opportunities fully. Organizations must implement policies that promote flexibility, parental leave, and supportive work environments to enable women to continue thriving professionally while balancing their responsibilities. By providing the necessary support systems, organizations can create a level playing field and ensure women have equal opportunities to advance and succeed.

The underrepresentation of women in specific industries and sectors is another roadblock to achieving gender parity. Some fields, such as STEM (Science, Technology, Engineering, and Mathematics), continue to have a significant gender imbalance, with women being underrepresented. This lack of representation stems from various factors, including societal stereotypes, limited access to education and resources, and workplace cultures that are unwelcoming or unsupportive for women. Organizations must actively promote diversity and inclusion in these fields by encouraging girls and women to pursue STEM education and careers, providing mentorship opportunities, and creating inclusive work environments that value and support women's contributions.

A lack of female role models and mentors in leadership positions poses another roadblock to gender parity. When women do not see others who look like them in senior roles, it can be challenging to envision themselves in similar positions. Organizations must prioritize developing and promoting female leaders and create mentorship programs that facilitate sharing of knowledge, experiences, and support between women at different stages of their careers. By fostering a strong network of role models and mentors, organizations can provide aspiring women leaders with the guidance and inspiration they need to navigate their professional journeys and overcome obstacles.

While progress has continued in achieving gender parity within organizations, significant roadblocks still hinder true equality. Overcoming unconscious biases, promoting work-life balance and support systems, addressing underrepresentation in specific industries, and fostering female role models and mentors are critical steps toward achieving gender parity. Organizations must continue to prioritize diversity and inclusion, implement policies that promote equal opportunities, and challenge societal norms and expectations. By breaking down these roadblocks, organizations can create a more inclusive and equitable environment where all individuals, regardless of gender, have the opportunity to thrive and contribute to their fullest potential.

Questions for Leadership Discussion

1. How do gender dynamics in leadership roles contribute to the underrepresentation of women in top leadership positions? What are some specific challenges women face in their journey to leadership?

2. What are the implications of gender biases and stereotypes in male-dominated and female-dominated organizational leadership structures? How do these biases hinder progress towards gender equality in leadership?

3. How can my/our organization challenge and dismantle gender biases and stereotypes in leadership? What strategies and initiatives can be implemented to create more inclusive environments that value diverse leadership styles?

4. What are some of the structural and systemic barriers that impede gender parity in my/our organization? How can these barriers be addressed and overcome to promote equal opportunities for women in leadership?

5. How does intersectionality impact women's experiences in leadership? How can my/our organization recognize and address the unique challenges faced by women from marginalized and underrepresented groups in their journey to leadership?

6. What are the consequences of a lack of gender diversity in leadership? How can my/our organization leverage the benefits of diverse perspectives and talents to enhance

decision-making, innovation, and overall organizational performance?

7. How do gender biases and stereotypes affect men in leadership roles, and why is it important to address these issues for both men and women?

8. What are some effective strategies and interventions my/our organization can implement to break down gender biases and stereotypes in leadership? How can education, awareness, and policy changes contribute to achieving gender parity?

9. What progress has been made in recent years towards gender equality in leadership? What are some success stories and best practices in promoting gender parity within my/our organization?

10. What are the remaining roadblocks and challenges in achieving true gender equality in leadership? How can my/our organization continue to prioritize diversity, inclusion, and equal opportunities to overcome these barriers?

CHAPTER SIX

Developing Tomorrow's Leaders: The Role of Higher Education

> *Higher education institutions play a crucial role in fostering minority leaders by providing opportunities, support, and resources to help individuals from marginalized communities develop their leadership potential.*

Higher education institutions play a crucial role in fostering the development of minority leaders by providing opportunities, support, and resources to help individuals from marginalized communities develop their leadership potential. However, even these institutions face the unparalleled task of examining internal diversity, equity, and inclusion practices. This critical responsibility aids in shaping the future of minority leaders by cultivating diversity and inclusion throughout the organization, including curriculum, policies, faculty, and staff representation. By offering a range of educational, support, and development opportunities, these institutions play a pivotal role in empowering minority individuals to thrive in leadership positions and positively impact future employers. Here are several vital functions that higher education institutions play in this regard:

The Role of Higher Education in Leadership Development

Access to education: Higher education institutions strive to provide equitable access to education for students from all backgrounds, including minority communities. By actively recruiting and admitting a diverse student body, institutions open doors for individuals who may have faced historical barriers to educational opportunities. This access to education serves as a foundation for minority students to develop the knowledge, skills, and competencies necessary for leadership roles.

Scholarships and financial support: Scholarships and financial support initiatives within higher education institutions play a pivotal role in breaking down barriers and fostering diversity and inclusivity. These programs go beyond their economic impact, serving as critical tools to address broader societal disparities and empower talented individuals from marginalized communities.

Financial constraints can often be a significant deterrent for aspiring students from minority backgrounds to pursue higher education. Scholarships, grants, and financial aid programs act as equalizers, leveling the playing field and creating opportunities for those who might otherwise face financial hurdles. By alleviating the financial burden of tuition fees, these initiatives empower minority students to embark on their academic journeys with purpose and determination, unburdened by the financial constraints that might have otherwise limited their prospects.

However, the impact of scholarships and financial support extends beyond financial relief. These programs convey to marginalized communities that their aspirations and potential are recognized and valued. It signals that institutions are actively invested in creating pathways for their success and advancement, fostering a sense of belonging and inclusivity. Such an environment encourages students to fully engage in their educational pursuits, unlocking their potential and enabling them to become future leaders.

Moreover, scholarships and financial support contribute to a broader transformation in society. By enabling minority students to access higher education, these initiatives contribute to a more diverse pool of graduates entering various professional fields. This diversity is essential for enriching perspectives, driving innovation, and dismantling systemic biases that have historically excluded marginalized groups. When minority students can overcome financial obstacles and pursue higher education, they align more favorably, positioning themselves as agents of change in their communities and fields of interest.

In essence, scholarships and financial support programs represent a tangible commitment by higher education institutions to create a more equitable society. Institutions are investing in the student's personal growth and broader societal advancement by offering avenues for talented individuals from marginalized communities to access education. Through financial support, institutions pave the way for future leaders who bring diverse perspectives, fresh ideas, and a commitment to positive change.

This commitment resonates beyond the campus, shaping a more inclusive and empowered future for all.

Mentoring and support programs: Mentoring and support programs within higher education institutions play a vital role in nurturing the growth and leadership development of minority students. These programs go beyond traditional academic guidance, offering a holistic approach that recognizes the multifaceted challenges students from marginalized backgrounds face. By connecting students with experienced mentors, these initiatives create a powerful support system that enhances academic success, personal growth, and leadership potential.

At their core, mentoring programs provide a bridge between classroom learning and real-world experiences. By pairing minority students with seasoned mentors, institutions create opportunities for meaningful connections that extend beyond the confines of the academic curriculum. Mentors, often professionals in relevant fields, offer insights, advice, and practical guidance that students can apply to their personal and professional lives. This mentor-student relationship fosters a sense of belonging and support essential for navigating the complexities of higher education and the transition into the workforce.

One of the significant advantages of mentoring programs is the tailored guidance they provide. Mentors understand the unique challenges that minority students might face related to identity, cultural adjustment, or career aspirations. As a result, mentors can offer personalized advice and strategies to help students overcome these challenges and thrive. This individualized support enhances academic performance and cultivates a sense of empowerment, resilience, and self-confidence among minority students.

Furthermore, mentoring programs contribute to a more comprehensive leadership development process. As mentors share their experiences, challenges, and triumphs, students gain valuable insights into various aspects of leadership, from effective communication to decision-making. This exposure equips minority students with a well-rounded skill set beyond academic achievements, positioning them as well-prepared leaders in their future careers.

Institutions prioritizing mentoring and support programs invest in their students' long-term success. These initiatives not only address the specific challenges faced by minority students but also contribute to a more inclusive campus culture. By creating spaces where students can openly discuss their concerns, aspirations, and goals, institutions send a powerful message that diverse perspectives are valued and essential. This message extends beyond graduation, influencing how minority students perceive their potential and contribute to society as future leaders.

Principally, mentoring and support programs act as catalysts for transformative growth. They provide minority students with the tools, guidance, and networks to overcome obstacles and reach their leadership potential. By fostering a nurturing and supportive environment, these initiatives enable minority students to excel academically, develop vital leadership skills, and emerge as empowered leaders ready to contribute positively to their communities and beyond.

Inclusive curriculum and diverse perspectives: An inclusive curriculum and integrating diverse perspectives are pivotal aspects of higher education institutions' efforts to foster a more inclusive and enlightened learning environment. By deliberately incorporating courses that delve into issues of race, ethnicity, gender, and social justice, institutions go beyond traditional educational boundaries to equip students with a comprehensive understanding of the complexities and realities faced by marginalized communities.

The significance of an inclusive curriculum lies in its ability to broaden students' horizons and challenge their preconceived notions. When students experience a range of perspectives, histories, and contributions from various cultural backgrounds, it encourages them to examine the world around them critically. This exposure fosters a deeper appreciation for diversity and a heightened awareness of societal systemic inequities. As a result, students are better equipped to engage in meaningful discussions about social justice, equality, and the experiences of marginalized groups.

Inclusive curricula also have a transformative impact on student's personal development. By exploring diverse narratives, students develop empathy and a heightened sensitivity to the challenges faced by individuals from different backgrounds. This empathy extends beyond the classroom, influencing their interactions, decision-making, and societal contributions. An inclusive curriculum nurtures individuals who are academically knowledgeable, socially conscious, and equipped to advocate for positive change.

Moreover, an inclusive curriculum plays a vital role in preparing future leaders to address the multifaceted challenges of our globalized world. As students engage with topics that intersect with issues of race, gender, and social justice, they develop critical thinking skills that are essential for effective leadership. These skills enable students to analyze complex problems from various angles, consider diverse perspectives, and make informed decisions that contribute to positive societal transformations.

By promoting an inclusive curriculum, higher education institutions send a powerful message about the value of diversity and the importance of acknowledging historically marginalized voices. This approach challenges the status quo and underscores the commitment to creating an environment where all students feel valued, represented, and empowered. Ultimately, an inclusive curriculum shapes the next generation of leaders who are academically adept, socially conscious, compassionate, and equipped to drive positive change in an increasingly interconnected and diverse world.

Leadership development programs: Leadership development programs within higher education institutions serve as transformative platforms that empower minority students with the skills, knowledge, and confidence needed to navigate leadership roles effectively. These programs go beyond traditional academic instruction, aiming to equip students with the practical tools to drive positive change within their communities and beyond.

One of the vital strengths of leadership development programs is their tailored approach to the unique challenges faced by minority students. Recognizing that individuals from marginalized backgrounds may encounter distinct barriers and opportunities, these programs are meticulously designed to address those needs. Participants comprehensively understand leadership dynamics through targeted workshops, hands-on experiences, and skill-building exercises while honing the skills necessary to excel in various contexts.

Moreover, these programs foster a supportive environment that encourages self-discovery and self-confidence. Through experiential learning, students engage in real-world scenarios, allowing them to apply theoretical knowledge to practical situations. This process hones their leadership skills and boosts their self-assurance as they witness their ability to effect change and contribute meaningfully.

Networking plays a pivotal role in leadership development programs. By facilitating connections with peers, mentors, and professionals, these programs provide students with access to diverse perspectives and experiences. Networking opportunities expand students' horizons and serve as a vital steppingstone for future career prospects. Building a robust network empowers minority students to access resources, mentorship, and potential leadership roles that might otherwise be challenging to attain.

At its core, leadership development for minority students is about fostering a sense of agency and responsibility. By equipping students with the tools to tackle real-world challenges, institutions empower them to advocate for change, whether it's within their local communities or on a broader societal scale. These programs enable students to recognize their potential as leaders who can drive progress and contribute meaningfully to addressing issues of inequality and injustice.

Leadership development programs tailored to minority students exemplify higher education institutions' commitment to fostering a diverse, equitable, and inclusive environment. Providing comprehensive training, boosting self-confidence, facilitating networking, and promoting active community engagement prepare minority students to be effective, empathetic, and impactful leaders who contribute positively to society. Through these initiatives, institutions contribute to their student's academic growth and advancement.

Representation and role modeling: Representation and role modeling within higher education institutions are crucial components in creating an environment that nurtures the leadership aspirations of minority students. These efforts go beyond numerical diversity; they actively cultivate a sense of belonging and provide tangible examples of success that resonate deeply with underrepresented individuals.

When students encounter faculty, staff, and administrators who share their racial, ethnic, or gender identity in leadership roles, it sends a powerful message of possibility and potential. The presence of diverse role models dismantles the notion that leadership is limited to a specific group, challenging stereotypes, and offering a new narrative of inclusivity. It affirms to minority students that their unique perspectives, experiences, and aspirations are valued and essential to their growth and success.

Representation and role modeling become pathways to relatability and inspiration. Seeing leaders who have navigated similar challenges and overcome similar barriers reassures students that they can achieve their goals. This inspiration extends beyond academic pursuits; it carries into every facet of students' lives, giving them the confidence to pursue leadership positions, engage in meaningful initiatives, and contribute to their communities.

Moreover, representation and role modeling contribute to a more holistic educational experience. Diverse leadership enriches classroom discussions, curriculum development, and institutional decision-making. Different perspectives foster critical thinking and encourage students to question established norms, promoting a dynamic and inclusive learning environment. By encountering a range of backgrounds and experiences among their leaders, students are better equipped to understand the complexities of a globalized world and to embrace diversity as a cornerstone of progress.

Institutions fostering strong minority representation and role modeling recognize the transformative potential of showcasing leadership from many backgrounds. They actively bridge the gap between possibility and reality for minority students by illustrating that leadership roles are within reach. As students witness individuals who mirror their identities succeeding in leadership capacities, a sense of belonging and empowerment flourishes. This representation cultivates a shared narrative that encourages aspiring leaders to push boundaries and redefine what is achievable.

Lastly, representation and role modeling are pivotal facets of higher education institutions' responsibility in fostering leadership among minority students. By elevating diverse leaders to positions of influence, institutions create an environment where all students, regardless of their background, can envision themselves as leaders. The presence of relatable role models sends a resounding message that leadership knows no bounds, setting the stage for a more inclusive, equitable, and empowered future.

Community engagement and partnerships: Community engagement and partnerships are integral pillars in higher education institutions' commitment to nurturing the growth of minority leaders. This strategic involvement with local communities and collaborative efforts with organizations dedicated to marginalized populations amplify the impact of education beyond the campus walls. By extending their reach and resources to these partnerships, institutions become catalysts for real-world change and developing resilient, empowered leaders.

Collaborating with community-based organizations presents a unique avenue to address the specific needs and aspirations of minority populations. These partnerships acknowledge that leadership is not confined to academic settings but plays a profound role in societal transformation. Higher education institutions tap into existing networks and trust by aligning with organizations serving these communities, establishing a solid mentorship, learning, and growth foundation.

Through such partnerships, institutions offer educational resources, practical training, and skills development. Workshops, seminars, and training sessions tailored to the challenges faced by minority leaders help individuals build a robust leadership toolkit. By recognizing the unique obstacles that minority leaders might encounter, these initiatives equip them with the strategies, confidence, and resilience needed to navigate complex situations and contribute effectively.

Furthermore, community engagement and partnerships provide a two-way learning experience. Institutions benefit from gaining insights into marginalized communities' lived experiences, needs, and aspirations, enriching the educational process with a deeper understanding of societal dynamics. In return, they contribute their expertise, resources, and mentorship to empower individuals from these communities to create lasting change.

Beyond academia, these collaborations build social cohesion and foster a sense of collective ownership. When higher education institutions and community organizations work together, they create a bridge between theory and practice, between aspirations and tangible outcomes. This synergy cultivates a shared vision for progress and empowers minority leaders to engage meaningfully in shaping the future of their communities.

Inherently, community engagement and partnerships amplify the transformative potential of higher education institutions. By extending their reach beyond the campus and collaborating with community-based organizations, institutions nurture a new generation of leaders who are not only well-equipped academically but also deeply connected to the needs and realities of their communities. These partnerships provide minority leaders with the tools, networks, and resources to lead purposefully and effect positive change on multiple levels. As higher education institutions continue to forge these meaningful connections, they contribute to a more inclusive and empowered society where leadership knows no boundaries.

Research and advocacy: Research and advocacy represent potent tools that higher education institutions can wield to drive meaningful change in the landscape of minority leadership. With their resources, expertise, and academic rigor, institutions can play a pivotal role in illuminating the challenges, opportunities, and best practices for advancing diversity, equity, and inclusion in leadership roles.

This endeavor's heart is research that delves into the complexities of underrepresentation and marginalization. By conducting rigorous studies and investigations, institutions generate data-driven insights that shed light on the barriers faced by minority leaders and the systemic factors that perpetuate inequities. This research raises awareness and provides a foundation for evidence-based policies and practices aimed at dismantling these barriers.

Through research, higher education institutions contribute to a broader understanding of the intersectional challenges faced by minority leaders. By exploring the nuanced ways in which factors such as race, gender, ethnicity, and socioeconomic background intersect, institutions enrich the discourse with multifaceted insights. This deep understanding is critical for developing strategies that resonate with the lived experiences of minority leaders, ensuring that solutions are contextually relevant and practical.

Research-driven advocacy goes hand in hand with generating knowledge. By translating research findings into actionable recommendations and policy proposals, institutions become advocates for change at the systemic level. This advocacy encompasses engaging with policymakers, industry leaders, and other stakeholders to champion the implementation of policies that promote diversity and inclusion in leadership roles. Institutions leverage their influence to effect meaningful shifts in organizational practices, recruitment strategies, and leadership development initiatives.

Furthermore, research and advocacy initiatives provide a platform for institutions to engage with the broader public discourse. Institutions raise societal awareness about the importance of diverse leadership by disseminating research findings through academic publications, conferences, and public forums. This engagement fosters a broader dialogue that challenges preconceptions, sparks conversations, and fosters a collective commitment to creating more inclusive leadership pathways.

By championing research-based practices, higher education institutions also model the values they advocate for. They demonstrate the power of evidence-based decision-making, encouraging other sectors to follow suit. Moreover, by aligning their research efforts with their educational mission, institutions empower their students with the tools to drive change in their future careers, amplifying the impact of their advocacy far beyond the campus.

In effect, research and advocacy initiatives enable higher education institutions to go beyond their traditional role as educators. They become beacons of knowledge, insight, and change that radiate beyond their walls and into the fabric of society. Through robust research, thoughtful advocacy, and strategic engagement, institutions contribute to reshaping the narrative of minority leadership, challenging systemic inequities, and championing a future where diverse voices lead the way.

In summary, higher education institutions foster minority leaders by providing access to education, offering scholarships and financial support, establishing mentoring and support programs, promoting inclusive curricula, providing leadership development initiatives, ensuring representation and role modeling, engaging with communities, conducting research, and advocating for systemic change. Through these roles, higher education institutions contribute significantly to nurturing the next generation of diverse and inclusive leaders who will shape our society for the better.

Analyzing Strategies for Inclusive Leadership Programs

Diverse Search and Selection Committees: Diversity in search and selection committees is a pivotal cornerstone in reshaping the leadership landscape within higher education institutions. These committees serve as gatekeepers, entrusted with identifying and appointing leaders who possess the requisite qualifications and are committed to diversity, equity, and inclusion.

The composition of these committees is instrumental in shaping the trajectory of leadership representation. Organizations proactively challenge the biases and assumptions that can inadvertently permeate the selection process by ensuring that these committees mirror the institution's diverse population. When committee members bring different genders, races, ethnicities, and backgrounds to the table, they get diverse perspectives that can offer a more holistic view of leadership potential.

Diverse search and selection committees check against the perpetuation of traditional stereotypes and biases that may unconsciously influence hiring decisions. By incorporating a spectrum of viewpoints, these committees become better equipped to recognize and assess the full range of leadership competencies. This comprehensive evaluation can lead to identifying candidates whose skills, experiences, and leadership styles align with the institution's commitment to fostering an inclusive environment.

Organizations can formalize this commitment by implementing policies and guidelines that mandate diverse representation on these committees. By doing so, institutions signal their dedication to dismantling existing barriers and fostering a leadership pipeline that mirrors the richness of their community. These policies underscore the importance of embracing various perspectives and experiences in the selection process and ensure that every candidate's potential is evaluated equally.

The presence of diverse search and selection committees also sends a powerful message to potential candidates. It communicates that the institution values and prioritizes diversity, creating a more attractive and inclusive environment for prospective leaders. Candidates from underrepresented backgrounds are more likely to view an institution favorably when they see evidence of inclusive hiring practices, encouraging them to consider leadership roles within the organization.

Ultimately, the impact of diverse search and selection committees extends far beyond the appointment of individual leaders. It contributes to a cultural shift within institutions that acknowledges the importance of diversity in the classroom and the highest decision-making echelons. By harnessing the collective wisdom of committee members who represent a range of experiences, organizations lay the groundwork for a more inclusive, innovative, and responsive leadership landscape that can effectively guide higher education institutions into a more equitable future.

Resource Allocation for Diversity and Inclusion Initiatives: Resource allocation for diversity and inclusion initiatives reflects an institution's commitment to nurturing inclusive leadership in higher education. Beyond mere compliance with federal mandates, distributing financial and organizational resources is a strategic investment in advancing underrepresented voices and perspectives.

At the heart of this allocation lies the recognition that fostering inclusive leadership requires proactive and intentional efforts. Scholarships and fellowships tailored for underrepresented students form a crucial pillar in this endeavor. Institutions eliminate a critical barrier that hinders diverse individuals from accessing higher education by providing financial support. These initiatives not only open doors of opportunity for those who might otherwise face exclusion but also signal to the broader community that the institution values diversity and is dedicated to cultivating a diverse leadership pipeline.

Allocating resources for research on diversity and inclusion demonstrates a commitment to informed decision-making.

Research generates evidence-based insights that help institutions understand the challenges faced by underrepresented individuals and identify effective strategies for fostering their leadership development. By funding research in this area, institutions contribute to academic discourse and the practical implementation of inclusive leadership practices.

Establishing dedicated offices or departments focused on diversity, equity, and inclusion underscores the institutional commitment to sustained change. These entities serve as a hub for advocacy, coordination, and implementation of initiatives that promote equitable opportunities for all academic community members. These offices drive the development of inclusive leadership programs and provide a centralized space for addressing concerns, amplifying voices, and fostering an environment where every individual can thrive.

Resource allocation is a visible demonstration of institutional values, and its impact extends beyond monetary considerations. It sends a clear message to students, faculty, staff, and stakeholders that the institution is actively investing in fostering a culture of inclusion and equity. This commitment catalyzes attracting and retaining diverse talent, enhancing institutional reputation, and contributing positively to the broader societal dialogue on diversity and inclusion.

Ultimately, resource allocation for diversity and inclusion initiatives aligns with an institution's core mission of education and enlightenment. It acknowledges diverse perspectives' role in enriching academic experiences, driving innovation, and advancing societal progress. By investing resources in inclusive leadership programs, institutions pave the way for a future where leadership genuinely represents the diverse world it seeks to serve, cultivating a more equitable and inclusive higher education landscape.

These strategies for inclusive leadership programs in higher education institutions are designed to address the barriers and challenges that impede diversity and inclusion within leadership positions. By implementing mentorship and sponsorship programs, institutions can provide support and guidance to aspiring leaders from underrepresented groups, helping them navigate the complexities of the leadership journey. Leadership development workshops and training programs foster awareness and skills necessary for inclusive leadership practices, equipping leaders with the tools to create diverse and inclusive environments.

Diverse search and selection committees contribute to more equitable hiring processes by challenging biases and stereotypes and promoting the selection of leaders who prioritize diversity and inclusion. By actively involving individuals from diverse backgrounds in decision-making, colleges and universities can ensure that different perspectives are considered, and opportunities are provided to candidates from underrepresented groups.

Finally, allocating resources for diversity and inclusion initiatives demonstrates an institution's commitment to fostering inclusive leadership. Institutions that invest in scholarships, research, and dedicated offices create a supportive infrastructure that promotes diversity, equity, and inclusion at all levels.

These strategies work together to cultivate a culture of inclusive leadership within higher education institutions. By breaking down barriers, providing support and training, and prioritizing diversity and inclusion, institutions can foster environments where all individuals have equal opportunities to succeed and contribute to advancing the institution's mission.

Challenges to Initiatives Supporting Minority Leaders

In the pursuit of fostering inclusive leadership programs within higher education institutions, the endeavor is accompanied by various challenges. These hurdles, though formidable, are not insurmountable. As institutions endeavor to create environments that empower and nurture minority leaders, they must grapple with issues such as resistance to change, limited resources, the need for sustained commitment, cultural sensitivities, and the pervasive impact of unconscious biases. This discussion delves into these challenges, offering insights into potential solutions that can pave the way for the successful implementation of initiatives supporting the growth and advancement of minority leaders.

Resistance to Change: Resistance to change can be a significant challenge when implementing inclusive leadership programs. Some individuals within the institution may be resistant to the idea of diversity and inclusion initiatives or may feel threatened by the shift in power dynamics.

Solution: Navigating resistance to change necessitates a practical approach centered on clear communication and active engagement. Effectively conveying the reasoning behind inclusive leadership initiatives and highlighting their direct contributions to the institution's goals and achievements is pivotal. Encouraging dialogue with stakeholders and providing platforms for open discussions to address any apprehensions or misunderstandings is key. Additionally, facilitating training and educational sessions on diversity and inclusion can enhance awareness and comprehension, thereby fostering a more receptive environment for individuals to welcome and embrace the changes.

Limited Resources: Limited financial and organizational resources can pose a challenge when implementing inclusive leadership programs. Institutions may need more money to support these initiatives or competing priorities that make allocating sufficient resources to support these initiatives difficult.

Solution: Resource constraints are a common challenge that higher education institutions may encounter when striving to establish and sustain inclusive leadership programs. To overcome these constraints and ensure the successful implementation of such programs, institutions can adopt a multi-faceted approach:

1. **External Funding and Collaborations:** Seek opportunities for external funding from government grants, private foundations, and corporate sponsorships that are aligned with the mission of promoting diversity and inclusion in leadership. Collaborating with external partners who share

a similar vision can provide additional financial support, expertise, and resources.

2. **Grant Writing and Proposals:** Establish a dedicated team or individual responsible for identifying and applying for grants that support initiatives related to diverse leadership. This could involve researching grant opportunities, crafting compelling proposals, and ensuring compliance with application requirements.

3. **Reprioritizing Budgets:** Evaluate existing budgets across departments and programs to identify areas where funds can be reallocated to support inclusive leadership efforts. This may involve reevaluating the importance of certain expenditures and redirecting funds to prioritize diversity and inclusion initiatives.

4. **Senior Leadership Engagement:** Engage senior leadership, including university presidents, deans, and provosts, in advocating for the allocation of resources to diversity and inclusion programs. Clearly articulate the long-term benefits of investing in inclusive leadership, such as improved institutional reputation, student success, and overall organizational performance.

5. **Stakeholder Collaboration:** Foster collaboration with various stakeholders, including faculty, staff, students, alumni, and community partners. Involve them in discussions about the significance of inclusive leadership and the potential impact it can have on the institution's reputation and success.

6. **Endowment and Fundraising Campaigns:** Consider launching targeted fundraising campaigns or endowment drives specifically focused on supporting diversity and inclusion initiatives, including inclusive leadership programs. Donors who value diversity and equity may be motivated to contribute to such efforts.

7. **Utilizing Existing Resources Creatively:** Maximize the utilization of existing resources, such as facilities, technology, and personnel, to support inclusive leadership programs. Identify areas where these resources can be leveraged to create meaningful and impactful experiences for minority leaders.

8. **Long-Term Planning:** Incorporate diversity and inclusion goals into the institution's long-term strategic planning. By integrating these objectives into the broader institutional vision, it becomes easier to secure sustainable resources over time.

9. **Impact Assessment:** Develop a framework to measure the impact and outcomes of inclusive leadership programs. Demonstrating positive outcomes, such as increased student success, improved organizational culture, and enhanced community engagement, can provide a compelling case for continued resource allocation.

Overcoming resource constraints to establish and maintain inclusive leadership programs requires a strategic, multi-pronged approach. By proactively seeking external funding, reprioritizing budgets, engaging senior leadership, collaborating with stakeholders, and creatively utilizing existing resources, institutions can pave the way for sustainable initiatives that foster diverse and inclusive leadership.

Lack of Buy-in and Support from Leadership: Without solid support from institutional leaders, implementing inclusive leadership programs can face significant challenges. Lack of buy-in or limited support may hinder the allocation of resources, impede decision-making processes, and create a lack of accountability for diversity and inclusion goals.

Solution: Gaining buy-in and support from institutional leaders is a critical step in successfully implementing inclusive leadership programs. Initiating this process early and forging a shared vision is essential. Begin by presenting comprehensive data, research findings, and real-world case studies that underscore the positive impact of diversity and inclusion within higher education contexts. This evidence-based approach can effectively demonstrate the tangible benefits of fostering an inclusive leadership culture.

Work closely with institutional leaders to co-create strategic plans tailored to the institution's unique context and goals. These plans outline specific and measurable objectives for promoting inclusive leadership, aligning them with the institution's broader mission. By setting clear goals, leaders can better grasp the outcomes they can expect and the transformative potential of embracing diversity and inclusion.

Another key strategy is building long-lasting relationships with influential figures within the institution who are deeply committed to diversity and inclusion. Identify individuals who hold sway within various departments and leverage their passion for inclusivity to build a network of advocates. These advocates can champion the cause of inclusive leadership, helping to generate momentum, foster open dialogues, and effect meaningful change from within.

Ultimately, securing buy-in and support from institutional leaders involves a strategic blend of evidence, collaboration, goal setting, and advocacy. By presenting a well-informed case for the value of diversity and inclusion, involving leaders in the planning process, and cultivating a network of passionate advocates, institutions can overcome challenges and create a firm foundation for successful inclusive leadership initiatives.

Sustaining Long-Term Commitment: Maintaining a long-term commitment to inclusive leadership programs can be challenging, mainly when initial enthusiasm wanes, or leadership changes occur within the institution.

Solution: To sustain long-term commitment, embedding diversity and inclusion into the institution's values, policies, and practices is crucial. Integrate diversity and inclusion initiatives into the institution's strategic plan, ensuring their prioritization alongside other institutional goals. Establish precise accountability mechanisms and metrics to track progress and hold individuals and departments responsible for inclusive leadership outcomes.

Engage in regular communication and reporting to demonstrate the ongoing commitment to diversity and inclusion and celebrate successes along the way.

Unconscious Bias and Stereotypes: Unconscious bias and stereotypes can persist despite implementing inclusive leadership programs, impacting decision-making processes and perpetuating inequality.

Solution: Addressing unconscious bias and stereotypes requires ongoing education and training. Offer workshops and training sessions that raise awareness about biases, provide strategies for bias mitigation, and promote inclusive decision-making. Foster an environment where individuals feel comfortable speaking up and challenging biases. Implement blind recruitment practices, where possible, to reduce the influence of unconscious bias during hiring processes. Regularly evaluate and update recruitment and selection criteria to ensure they are inclusive and equitable.

Overcoming these challenges requires strategic planning, effective communication, stakeholder engagement, and a commitment to continuous improvement. By proactively addressing these challenges, higher education institutions can create environments that foster inclusive leadership, support diverse talent, and promote equal opportunities for all.

Challenges to Supporting Minority Leaders at PWIs

Implementing inclusive leadership programs in predominantly white institutions (PWIs) may present additional challenges due to the historical and systemic issues of racial inequality and underrepresentation. Even now in the 21st Century, minority students and employees of predominately white institutions find themselves experiencing microaggressions and discriminatory practices. Here are some specific challenges that PWIs may face and potential solutions to address them:

Lack of Representation and Diversity: PWIs often have a limited representation of racial and ethnic minorities in leadership positions, which can hinder the effectiveness of inclusive leadership programs. The lack of diverse role models and mentors can make it challenging for underrepresented students to envision themselves in leadership roles.

Solution: Predominantly White Institutions (PWIs) must proactively enhance diversity within their leadership teams. This enhancement involves a concerted effort to recruit, hire, and advance individuals from underrepresented backgrounds. To achieve this, PWIs should implement robust strategies for identifying and attracting talented candidates from diverse communities, both internally and externally.

One approach is to refine the recruitment process to ensure it is inclusive and actively seeks candidates from underrepresented groups. This approach could involve partnering with professional organizations and networks focusing on diversity and connecting with a broader range of potential candidates. Additionally, expanding the outreach of job postings and utilizing platforms that target diverse talent pools can help attract a more varied applicant pool.

Institutional leaders should also assess and address potential biases in the hiring and promotion process. This assessment might involve implementing anonymous application reviews, where candidate names and demographic information remain concealed during the initial evaluation. Training search and selection committees on recognizing unconscious biases and evaluating candidates solely on their qualifications can lead to more equitable outcomes.

Creating a transparent and merit-based advancement system is crucial. When individuals from underrepresented backgrounds perceive clear pathways for growth and opportunities, they are more likely to engage fully and invest in their careers. Establishing performance benchmarks, providing regular feedback, and offering professional development resources can facilitate the career progression of diverse individuals within the institution.

By focusing on recruitment strategies that actively seek out diverse candidates, address unconscious biases, and foster transparent advancement opportunities, PWIs can make significant strides toward diversifying their leadership teams and promoting a more inclusive and equitable environment.

Institutional Culture and Climate: PWIs may have institutional cultures perpetuating bias, racism, and exclusion, creating a challenging environment for inclusive leadership initiatives. Unaddressed racial biases and discriminatory practices can undermine efforts to create an inclusive and equitable leadership culture.

Solution: PWIs must actively cultivate a culture of diversity and inclusion by instituting structural changes and promoting ongoing awareness. One practical approach is establishing clear and transparent anti-racist policies and practices that guide behavior and decision-making across the institution. This approach entails not only addressing overt racism but also proactively dismantling systemic barriers that perpetuate inequality.

Creating safe spaces for open dialogue about race and racism is crucial. Initiatives such as town hall meetings, forums, and diversity-focused events encourage authentic conversations that increase understanding and empathy. These platforms allow individuals to share their experiences, express concerns, and collaborate on solutions.

Furthermore, leadership must model the values of diversity and inclusion by actively participating in and endorsing inclusive initiatives. When leaders visibly demonstrate their commitment to anti-racist practices, it sets a powerful example for the entire institution. Leaders can actively demonstrate their commitment through public statements, engagement in diversity events, and involvement in projects to address systemic disparities.

It's important to note that fostering a diverse and inclusive environment requires continuous effort and evaluation. Governing bodies for the organization should conduct regular assessments of the institution's progress in implementing anti-discriminatory policies and creating an inclusive atmosphere. By focusing on these structural changes and creating platforms for open dialogue, PWIs can work towards fostering an environment where all individuals feel respected, valued, and included.

Power Dynamics and Resistance to Change: Power dynamics within PWIs can challenge inclusive leadership programs. Resistance to change and preserving existing hierarchies may impede efforts to promote diversity and inclusion in leadership positions.

Solution: A practical solution to resistance to organizational change when implementing diversity and inclusion initiatives is to create a clear and compelling narrative highlighting the tangible benefits of these initiatives for the organization and its individual members. Senior leadership must lead the communication of this narrative consistently and transparently throughout the organization.

Clearly articulating how diversity and inclusion will enhance innovation, creativity, and problem-solving and contribute to better employee engagement and overall performance can help employees understand the positive impact on their work environment and career prospects.

Additionally, providing concrete examples of successful diversity and inclusion initiatives from other organizations or industries can help overcome skepticism. These success stories can illustrate the practical outcomes and demonstrate that the changes proposed are achievable and have been effective elsewhere.

Engaging in open dialogue and active listening is also vital. Leaders should create forums where employees can express their concerns, ask questions, and provide input. Addressing these concerns directly and honestly can help alleviate fears and build trust. Acknowledging that change can be challenging and committing to providing the necessary resources and support can reassure employees that their well-being and professional growth remain a priority.

The key is to craft a compelling narrative that resonates with employees' values and interests, backed by concrete evidence and transparent communication. This approach can reduce resistance and generate support for diversity and inclusion initiatives throughout the organization.

Building Trust and Authentic Relationships: Building trust between underrepresented students and institutional leaders can be challenging due to historical and ongoing racial inequities. Establishing authentic relationships based on mutual respect and understanding is crucial for the success of inclusive leadership programs.

Solution: Institutional leaders should proactively engage with underrepresented students, staff, and faculty communities, demonstrating their commitment to diversity and inclusion. Active engagement can involve reaching out directly to these communities, conducting one-on-one conversations, and participating in smaller group discussions. By actively listening to their concerns, experiences, and suggestions, leaders can gain insights into these individuals' challenges and identify targeted solutions.

In addition to engaging with individuals, leaders can collaborate with existing student organizations and initiatives that promote diversity and inclusion. By fostering partnerships, leaders can support and amplify the efforts of these groups, demonstrating solidarity and a shared commitment to positive change. This collaboration can lead to joint initiatives, events, and programs that help create a more inclusive environment.

To deepen their understanding of diverse perspectives, leaders should participate in cultural events, workshops, and programs that educate them about different backgrounds, histories, and experiences. This active involvement shows a genuine willingness to learn and empathize with underrepresented communities. It also sends a powerful message that leaders are committed to fostering an inclusive environment where everyone's voice is valued.

Ultimately, these actions help leaders build trust and credibility within underrepresented communities, signaling a sincere dedication to meaningful change. By engaging directly with these communities, partnering with existing initiatives, and participating in educational opportunities, leaders can contribute to a more inclusive campus culture.

Addressing challenges in PWIs require a comprehensive and sustained commitment from institutional leaders, faculty, staff, and students. It is paramount to recognize that addressing racial inequities and promoting inclusive leadership is an ongoing process that requires continuous learning, collaboration, and accountability. By taking proactive steps to address these challenges, PWIs can work towards creating more inclusive and equitable leadership environments that empower all individuals to succeed.

Key University Initiatives Supporting Minority Leaders

While it is difficult to identify a top four or five list of university initiatives supporting minority leaders worldwide, several notable programs and initiatives implemented by universities worldwide support and empower minority leaders. Here are four examples:

Leadership Development Programs: Many universities offer programs specifically designed for minority students. These programs provide comprehensive training, mentorship, and networking opportunities to develop their leadership skills and advance their career. These initiatives often focus on fostering diversity, equity, and inclusion and provide specialized resources to address the unique challenges faced by minority leaders.

An example of a leadership development program for minority students is the Multicultural Leadership Program at the University of California, Berkeley. This program seeks to cultivate the leadership potential of students from underrepresented backgrounds and empower them to impact their communities positively and beyond.

The Multicultural Leadership Program provides participants with a comprehensive training curriculum that includes workshops, seminars, and skill-building sessions. These sessions cover various aspects of leadership, such as communication, teamwork, conflict resolution, and strategic planning. The program also offers mentorship opportunities, where students partner with experienced professionals who provide guidance and support throughout their leadership journey.

One of the key strengths of this program is its focus on diversity, equity, and inclusion. It recognizes and addresses the unique challenges faced by minority leaders, including systemic barriers and biases. Through specialized resources and discussions, the program creates a safe and supportive space for participants to explore and navigate these challenges.

The program also emphasizes networking and community engagement. Students have the opportunity to connect with a diverse network of peers, alums, and professionals from various industries. These connections provide valuable networking opportunities and foster a sense of community and support among participants.

By participating in the Multicultural Leadership Program, students gain the necessary skills, knowledge, and confidence to take on leadership roles in their academic, professional, and personal lives. The program equips them with the tools to challenge existing systems, advocate for equity and inclusivity, and become catalysts for positive change in their communities. It's worth noting that this is just one example, and there are numerous other leadership development programs for minority students offered by universities worldwide. Each program may have its unique approach and focus areas, but they all share the goal of empowering minority leaders and promoting diversity, equity, and inclusion in leadership positions.

Scholarships and Fellowships: Universities worldwide offer scholarships and fellowships targeted explicitly toward minority students to promote their participation in leadership roles. These financial aid programs aim to reduce barriers and provide opportunities for underrepresented individuals to pursue higher education, gain leadership skills, and contribute to their communities. These initiatives help in increasing representation and diversity in leadership positions.

An example of a scholarship and fellowship program for minority students outside of the United States is the Rhodes Scholarship. Established in 1902, the Rhodes Scholarship is one of the most prestigious international scholarship programs awarded to exceptional students from various countries.

The Rhodes Trust offers the Rhodes Scholarship, allowing students from eligible countries to pursue postgraduate studies at the University of Oxford in the United Kingdom. The scholarship aims to nurture future leaders by providing them with a transformative educational experience and opportunities for personal and intellectual growth.

The scholarship is open to students from different backgrounds, including minority groups, who have demonstrated outstanding academic achievement, leadership potential, and a commitment to positively impacting the world. Recipients of the Rhodes Scholarship receive full financial support for their studies at Oxford, including tuition fees, a living stipend, and additional allowances.

Beyond financial support, the Rhodes Scholarship offers a robust leadership development program. Scholars can access mentoring, networking opportunities, and leadership and social change seminars. They are encouraged to engage in extracurricular activities, pursue community service projects, and contribute to public life during their time at Oxford.

The Rhodes Scholarship has significantly promoted diversity and representation in leadership positions by providing exceptional minority students with the resources and support they need to excel academically and develop their leadership potential. Many Rhodes Scholars have become influential leaders in their respective fields, contributing to positive change and making a difference in their communities and beyond.

There have been many notable minority recipients of the Rhodes Scholarship throughout its history. Cory Booker, an American politician and U.S. Senator from New Jersey was awarded the Rhodes Scholarship in 1992. He studied at the University of

Oxford and earned a Bachelor of Arts degree in Modern History. Booker has since had a successful political career, serving as the mayor of Newark, New Jersey, and later as a senator.

Additionally, Myron Rolle, a retired NFL player, received the Rhodes Scholarship in 2008 during his senior year at Florida State University. Rolle, who played safety, decided to forgo his final year of college football to pursue a master's degree in medical anthropology at the University of Oxford as a Rhodes Scholar. His achievement garnered significant attention and recognition as he balanced his academic pursuits with a promising football career. Rolle has earned his medical degree and engaged in medical and philanthropic endeavors, including Neurosurgery Residency at Harvard Medical School and Massachusetts General Hospital.

While the Rhodes Scholarship is just one example of an international scholarship and fellowship program that supports minority students in their pursuit of higher education and leadership development, many universities around the world offer similar initiatives aimed at increasing diversity, representation, and inclusivity in leadership roles through financial aid and comprehensive support programs.

Affinity and Support Groups: Many universities establish affinity and support groups for minority students to create a sense of belonging, provide mentorship, and offer a platform for networking and collaboration. These groups bring together individuals from similar backgrounds, identities, or interests and often organize events, workshops, and seminars to empower and support minority leaders. These initiatives foster a supportive community and help individuals build essential networks for career advancement.

A highly recognized affinity and support group for minority students is the Black Student Union (BSU). The BSU aims to create a sense of belonging and community for Black students on campus while providing them with resources and opportunities for personal and professional growth. The first Black Student Union (BSU) was started in 1966 at San Francisco State College (now San Francisco State University) in the United States as a response to racial inequalities and the lack of representation and support for Black students on campus. The formation of this BSU marked an important milestone in the history of student activism and the Black Power movement, as it advocated for academic and social changes to address the needs and concerns of Black students.

The establishment of the BSU at San Francisco State College also inspired the creation of similar affinity groups on college and university campuses across the United States, including Asian American organizations, Latinx student groups, and LGBTQ+ organizations. These groups provide a platform for students to connect with individuals with similar backgrounds or identities, fostering a sense of solidarity and support within the university community.

The BSU organizes various events and programs throughout the academic year, including guest speaker series, workshops, and cultural celebrations. These events allow students to engage in meaningful discussions, share their experiences, and connect. The BSU collaborates with other student organizations and campus departments to address diversity, equity, and inclusion issues. Most notably, mentorship is a crucial component of the BSU. The organization pairs incoming students with peer mentors who can provide guidance, support, and advice on navigating campus life and academic pursuits. The mentors also serve as role models for aspiring minority leaders and offer insights into leadership opportunities on and off campus.

Establishing affinity and support groups at universities like San Francisco State University significantly creates inclusive and empowering environments for minority students, faculty, and staff. Colleges and universities committed to real change will not placate affinity groups through symbolic posturing and traditional rhetoric. Establishing an environment that fosters a real sense of belonging, mentorship, and opportunities for collaboration, these groups contribute to the development and success of minority leaders, equipping them with the skills and networks needed for future leadership roles.

Diversity and Inclusion Initiatives: Universities worldwide implement comprehensive diversity and inclusion initiatives to support minority leaders. These initiatives encompass a range of strategies, such as establishing diversity and inclusion offices, implementing bias training programs, conducting cultural competency workshops, and creating inclusive policies and practices. These efforts aim to cultivate an inclusive and equitable environment that promotes the success and advancement of minority leaders.

An international example of a higher education institution implementing diversity and inclusion initiatives to support minority leaders is the University of Toronto in Canada. The university has established the Anti-Racism & Cultural Diversity Office (ARCDO) to foster an inclusive campus environment. ARCDO works to promote diversity, equity, and inclusion through various programs and initiatives.

One key initiative ARCDO offers is the Anti-Racism and Cultural Diversity Training Program. This program provides training and workshops for faculty, staff, and students to enhance their understanding of systemic racism, unconscious bias, and cultural diversity. The training aims to develop participants' cultural competence, empathy, and awareness of the experiences and challenges faced by minority individuals and communities.

The University of Toronto also hosts annual events and campaigns celebrating diversity and promoting inclusivity. For example, the "My First Time" campaign encourages individuals to share their experiences as first-generation, international, or students from marginalized backgrounds. This initiative aims to highlight and recognize students' diverse journeys and perspectives, fostering a sense of belonging and understanding on campus.

By implementing comprehensive diversity and inclusion initiatives that include diverse representation in leadership positions, implementing fair hiring practices, and providing resources and support for underrepresented groups, the University of Toronto demonstrates its commitment to creating an inclusive and equitable environment for minority leaders. These initiatives provide support and resources and promote awareness, understanding, and respect for the diverse experiences and contributions of all individuals within the university community.

Key Legislative Initiatives Impacting DEI Practices

In the United States, DEI initiatives have been a subject of controversy in some states, with specific lawmakers and groups expressing opposition to them. In contrast, others support and advocate for such initiatives to promote equality and inclusivity.

In Texas, Senate Bill 17 (S.B. 17) aims to target certain Diversity, Equity, and Inclusion (DEI) practices at public institutions of higher education. The bill prohibits universities from establishing or maintaining DEI offices, officers, employees, or contractors that perform the duties of a DEI office. It also prohibits requiring specific training and ideological oaths related to diversity, equity, and inclusion. The legislation seeks to ensure that institutions do not give preferential consideration based on race, sex, color, ethnicity, or national origin during employment or any institutional functions.

S.B. 17 also states that certain sections do not apply to academic course instruction, scholarly research, student organization activities, guest speakers, policies promoting student achievement regardless of race or ethnicity, data collection, student recruitment, or admissions. The bill mandates that the governing board of each institution testifies before legislative committees about compliance with the bill. The state auditor will periodically conduct compliance audits, and non-compliance with the bill may lead to funding restrictions for institutions.

As described in the previous paragraph, S.B. 17 appears to limit certain Diversity, Equity, and Inclusion (DEI) practices at public institutions of higher education in Texas. Whether or not it conflicts with America's historic pattern of racism and discriminatory practices is a matter of interpretation and perspective; however, given recent Supreme Court rulings on affirmative action and the reversal of Roe v. Wade, strong arguments can be made supporting the continuation of racial and discriminatory practices under the guise and protection of legal proceedings.

Some argue that the bill's restrictions on DEI practices could serve as a mechanism to support the departure from efforts to address historical racial and discriminatory injustices. Initiatives promoting diversity, equity, and inclusion have often received support as necessary steps to rectify the legacy of racism and discrimination that has affected marginalized communities throughout American history.

On the other hand, proponents of the bill may argue that it seeks to ensure equal treatment for all individuals, regardless of their race, sex, color, ethnicity, or national origin, and that the bill aims to prevent preferential treatment based on these characteristics. They may contend that promoting a color-blind approach is the most equitable way to address historical injustices and create a level playing field for all.

Ultimately, assessing whether this bill conflicts with America's historic pattern of racism and discriminatory practices will depend on individual perspectives and the broader context of its implementation. It is essential to consider diverse viewpoints and engage in open and informed discussions to understand the implications and potential consequences of such legislation fully.

The bill, as summarized, does not explicitly mention specific underlying socioeconomic factors. However, discussions around Diversity, Equity, and Inclusion (DEI) initiatives in education often touch upon various socioeconomic factors that can influence representation and opportunities for marginalized communities. Some of the underlying socioeconomic factors that may not be directly addressed in the bill but are relevant to DEI discussions in education include:

1. **Economic Disparities:** Socioeconomic status can significantly impact access to quality education, resources, and opportunities. Low-income communities may face challenges related to educational attainment, access to technology, and college affordability, affecting their representation in higher education and leadership roles.

2. **Educational Disparities:** Historically disadvantaged communities might face inequities in K-12 education, leading to educational gaps and reduced opportunities for higher education. Addressing disparities in early education can influence diversity in higher education leadership positions.

3. **Access to Support Services:** Minority students may require additional support services, such as mentoring, counseling, or financial aid, to succeed in higher education. Lack of access to such services can hinder their chances of assuming leadership roles.

4. **Cultural Barriers:** Cultural norms and expectations within specific communities may impact their perceptions of leadership and career choices. Encouraging diversity in leadership requires understanding and addressing these cultural barriers.

5. **Unconscious Bias:** Unconscious biases can influence recruitment, hiring, and promotion decisions, leading to the underrepresentation of certain groups in leadership roles.

6. **Workplace Discrimination:** Even if educational opportunities are improved, workplace discrimination can hinder the advancement of minority individuals into leadership positions.

7. **Community Networks and Opportunities:** Access to professional networks and opportunities can differ based on socioeconomic backgrounds, impacting career progression.

8. **Health Disparities:** Socioeconomic factors can influence health disparities, affecting overall well-being and potential for academic and professional success.

It is essential to recognize that DEI efforts should consider and address these underlying socioeconomic factors to create more comprehensive and effective strategies for promoting diversity and inclusion in leadership positions. While the bill may focus on specific aspects of DEI initiatives in higher education, these socioeconomic factors are critical in shaping opportunities and outcomes for marginalized communities.

The initiatives and laws supporting the development of minority leaders can vary significantly from one university to another and are influenced by regional or national contexts. The effectiveness of these initiatives also depends on the resources, commitment, and collaboration of the university and its stakeholders. Therefore, it is essential for universities to continually assess and refine their programs to ensure they meet the evolving needs of emerging minority stakeholders and contribute to their success.

Questions for Leadership Discussion

1. How do higher education institutions address the historical barriers to educational opportunities faced by minority students in their efforts to foster diversity and inclusion in leadership positions?

2. What role do mentorship and support programs play in empowering minority students to thrive in leadership positions, and how do they contribute to their personal and professional growth?

3. How can higher education institutions effectively incorporate inclusive curricula that highlight diverse perspectives, histories, and contributions to nurture future leaders who are equipped to address complex social issues?

4. What are the key challenges of higher education institutions in implementing and sustaining diversity and inclusion initiatives to support minority leaders, and what strategies can be employed to overcome these challenges?

CHAPTER SEVEN

Navigating Organizational Challenges: Building Supportive Cultures

> ❝
>
> *Addressing structural bias requires a comprehensive and ongoing commitment to creating inclusive systems, policies, and practices that provide equal opportunities for all individuals, regardless of their background or identity.*

Systemic barriers significantly impede the progress of minority leaders, presenting substantial challenges to their advancement in various sectors. These barriers are rooted in social structures, policies, and practices and create unequal opportunities that hinder the realization of diverse leadership. Among the key systemic barriers is structural bias, leading to discriminatory hiring and promotion practices and limited representation, causing minority leaders to feel invisible and excluded from leadership roles. Additionally, limited access to networks, implicit bias, and stereotypes restrict their professional growth, impeding their access to resources, mentorship, and funding. Addressing these barriers necessitates organizations' commitment to inclusive systems, policies, and practices, promoting diverse representation, establishing equitable networks, and providing training to combat biases. By breaking down these obstacles, we can cultivate an environment where the full potential of minority leaders is recognized, enabling them to thrive and contribute to organizational success.

Systemic Barriers Impeding Minority Leadership Progress

Systemic barriers can significantly impede the progress of minority leaders, posing significant challenges to their advancement in various sectors. These barriers are deeply ingrained in social structures, policies, and practices, creating unequal opportunities and hindering the full realization of diverse leadership. Here are six leading systemic barriers that impede minority leadership progress:

Structural Bias: Structural bias is a deeply rooted form of discrimination that exists within the structures and processes of organizations and institutions. It refers to the systemic barriers and prejudices that disadvantage minority individuals throughout various stages of their professional journeys, particularly in hiring and promotion practices.

Historically, the criteria and expectations set for leadership positions manifest structural bias. Traditional leadership stereotypes, often influenced by societal norms and historical prejudices, tend to favor individuals who conform to specific characteristics, such as being assertive, confident, and strong. These biases may unintentionally exclude individuals who do not fit these preconceived notions, including many talented minority leaders with different but equally valuable leadership qualities.

In hiring processes, unconscious biases can impact decision-making, leading to selecting candidates who closely align with the prevailing norms and expectations. For example, interviewers may unconsciously associate certain traits or experiences with leadership potential, favoring candidates with similar backgrounds or attributes. These associations perpetuate the underrepresentation of minority leaders, as they often find themselves evaluated against criteria inherently biased toward the dominant culture or majority group.

Promotion practices also suffer from structural bias, as decision-makers may rely on subjective assessments and informal networks that inadvertently favor individuals already in positions of power. These actions can create a cycle of exclusion, where minority leaders become excluded from advancement opportunities due to their limited visibility and access to influential networks. Consequently, they face barriers in progressing to higher-level positions, limiting their opportunities for growth and impact.

Organizations must critically examine their systems, policies, and procedures to address structural bias to identify and rectify discriminatory practices. Their process may involve:

- Implementing diversity and inclusion initiatives that promote fair and unbiased decision-making.
- Challenging traditional leadership stereotypes.
- Establishing transparent and inclusive promotion criteria.

Organizations can also invest in unconscious bias training to raise awareness among decision-makers and create a more equitable evaluation process.

Fostering diverse representation in leadership roles is crucial for combating structural bias. By actively seeking and promoting talented minority leaders, organizations can challenge the status quo and demonstrate their commitment to inclusivity. Diverse leadership teams bring varied perspectives, insights, and problem-solving approaches, enhancing creativity, innovation, and decision-making effectiveness.

Furthermore, organizations can leverage data and analytics to identify patterns of bias and measure progress toward reducing structural barriers. Regularly reviewing recruitment and promotion practices and conducting diversity audits can help identify areas for improvement and inform targeted strategies to create a more equitable and inclusive environment.

Addressing structural bias requires a comprehensive and ongoing commitment to creating inclusive systems, policies, and practices that provide equal opportunities for all individuals, regardless of their background or identity. By dismantling these biases, organizations can cultivate an environment where the full potential of minority leaders is recognized and valued, enabling them to thrive and contribute to organizational success.

Lack of Representation: The lack of representation of minority leaders in leadership positions is a significant barrier that impedes their progress. When individuals from underrepresented communities do not see people who share their backgrounds and experiences in positions of power and influence, it becomes challenging for them to envision themselves in those roles. This lack of representation can create a sense of invisibility and undermine the confidence and aspirations of aspiring minority leaders.

Visible role models and mentors are crucial in inspiring and guiding individuals on their leadership journey. They provide valuable insights, advice, and support based on their own experiences, which can help aspiring minority leaders navigate the complexities of career advancement. However, when diverse representation is absent, it becomes more challenging for aspiring leaders to find relatable role models who can provide them with the necessary guidance and mentorship.

The absence of representation also perpetuates the perception that leadership positions are not accessible or welcoming for minorities. When individuals from underrepresented communities do not see people who look like them in leadership roles, they may question their capabilities and wonder if their perspectives and contributions will be valued. This lack of representation can create a sense of exclusion and discourage aspiring minority leaders from pursuing leadership opportunities.

Furthermore, the lack of representation in leadership positions can result in limited access to networks and opportunities for advancement. Networks and informal connections often play a significant role in career progression, providing access to information, resources, and influential decision-makers. When minority leaders face underrepresentation, they may face challenges in accessing these networks, which can hinder their ability to secure essential opportunities, sponsorships, or mentorship.

To address the need for more representation, organizations must prioritize diversity and inclusion at all levels of leadership. Prioritizing cultural diversity includes:

- Actively seeking out and promoting individuals from underrepresented communities.
- Creating opportunities for their visibility.
- Ensuring their voices are heard and valued.

Organizations can establish mentorship programs that specifically connect aspiring minority leaders with successful leaders who share similar backgrounds, experiences, and challenges.

Additionally, it is essential to establish inclusive recruitment and promotion practices that actively seek out diverse talent and create equitable pathways to leadership positions. Setting these practices may involve removing biases from job descriptions and criteria, implementing blind recruitment processes, and providing unconscious bias training to decision-makers.

By increasing representation, organizations send a powerful message that leadership is accessible and achievable for individuals from all backgrounds. Diverse representation not only provides role models and mentors for aspiring minority leaders but also enriches decision-making processes, fosters innovation, and improves the overall effectiveness of organizations.

Ultimately, breaking the cycle of lack of representation requires intentional efforts to create inclusive environments where minority leaders can thrive. By addressing this systemic barrier, organizations can cultivate a diverse and inclusive leadership landscape that benefits individuals, organizations, and connected communities.

Limited Access to Networks: Limited access to networks is a significant barrier that hampers the progress of minority leaders. Networks and connections provide valuable opportunities for career advancement, including access to mentorship, sponsorship, job openings, and influential decision-makers. However, minority leaders often face challenges in accessing these networks, which can hinder their professional growth and limit their opportunities for promotion.

Exclusive networks, often formed through existing power structures, perpetuate the underrepresentation of diverse voices and perspectives in leadership circles. These networks may inadvertently favor individuals who already hold positions of privilege and exclude minorities, further marginalizing their voices and limiting their visibility and influence. The lack of diversity within networks can create an echo chamber where the reinforcement of similar perspectives stifles innovation and perpetuates systemic biases.

Limited network access can result in missed opportunities for minority leaders to showcase their skills, expertise, and potential. Without the connections and relationships from being part of influential networks, minority leaders may face challenges in accessing information about job openings, industry trends, and leadership development opportunities. This lack of access can hinder their ability to seize growth opportunities and make meaningful contributions within their organizations and industries.

To overcome this barrier, organizations and institutions must actively foster inclusive networks that provide equal access and opportunities for all individuals, regardless of their backgrounds. Access involves creating spaces and platforms facilitating networking, collaboration, and knowledge-sharing among diverse groups. It may also include establishing formal mentoring programs that connect minority leaders with influential individuals who can provide guidance and support.

In addition, organizations can promote diversity and inclusion within existing networks by challenging exclusive practices and actively seeking out diverse perspectives. Promoting diversity can be achieved through initiatives such as diversifying guest speakers, panelists, and conference participants, intentionally inviting and including individuals from underrepresented backgrounds in networking events, and encouraging cross-functional collaborations that bridge different networks and bring together individuals with diverse experiences and expertise.

Furthermore, organizations can support the development of external networks for minority leaders, such as affinity groups or professional associations that focus on specific minority communities or industries. These networks allow individuals to connect with peers, share experiences, access resources, and advocate for their collective interests.

By addressing the limited access to networks, organizations can create a more inclusive and equitable environment where minority leaders have equal opportunities to build connections, expand their influence, and contribute to their fullest potential. By diversifying networks, organizations can tap into a broader range of perspectives, ideas, and talents, leading to enhanced innovation, better decision-making, and increased organizational success.

Implicit Bias and Stereotypes: Implicit bias and stereotyping are significant barriers that impede the progress of minority leaders. Implicit bias is an individual's unconscious attitude and assumptions towards specific groups, often shaped by societal stereotypes and cultural conditioning. These biases can influence decision-making processes, leading to biased evaluations, lower expectations, and restricted opportunities for minority leaders.

Stereotypes based on race, ethnicity, gender, or other identities can have a detrimental impact on the advancement of minority leaders. These stereotypes can perpetuate negative assumptions, such as the belief that certain groups are less competent, less capable of leadership, or not suited for particular roles. As a result, minority leaders may face biased evaluations and the unofficial requirement to adhere to higher performance standards than their non-minority counterparts.

Implicit bias and stereotyping undermine the recognition of merit and potential among minority individuals. Their abilities, qualifications, and achievements may be overshadowed or undervalued due to preconceived notions and assumptions. These biases can lead to limited access to leadership opportunities, unequal pay, and a lack of recognition for their contributions.

To address implicit bias and stereotyping, organizations and institutions must take proactive measures to raise awareness, promote diversity, and challenge biases. Managing these proclivities includes providing training and education on unconscious bias to help individuals recognize and mitigate their predilections. Individuals can strive for fair and objective evaluations and decision-making processes by understanding the impact of bias and stereotypes.

Establishing inclusive policies and practices that promote equal opportunities for all individuals, irrespective of their backgrounds, is also crucial. Organizations should implement standardized evaluation criteria, clear performance expectations, and transparent promotion processes to minimize the influence of bias. Additionally, diverse selection committees and panels can help ensure the consideration of multiple perspectives during recruitment, performance assessments, and promotion decisions.

Creating a culture of inclusivity and respect is vital in combating implicit bias and stereotyping. Creating an inclusive culture involves fostering an environment where individuals feel comfortable challenging biases and stereotypes and where diverse perspectives are valued and encouraged. Organizations should prioritize diversity and inclusion in their mission, values, and strategic goals, clearly conveying that they will not tolerate bias and discrimination.

Furthermore, organizations can promote diverse representation in leadership positions, as having minority leaders in decision-making roles can help challenge stereotypes, dismantle biases, and serve as role models for aspiring minority leaders. When individuals see leaders who share their backgrounds and experiences, it can inspire confidence, motivation, and ambition, breaking the cycle of limited representation.

By addressing implicit bias and stereotyping, organizations can create more inclusive and equitable environments where minority leaders are evaluated based on merit, skills, and qualifications. This approach benefits individuals, enhances organizational performance, fosters innovation, and promotes a culture of fairness and equality.

Unequal Access to Resources and Opportunities: Unequal access to resources and opportunities is a significant barrier that hinders the progress of minority leaders. This disparity can manifest in various ways, including limited access to quality education, training programs, mentorship, and funding.

Access to quality education is a fundamental determinant of career advancement. However, minority individuals often face systemic barriers that limit their access to quality education. Factors such as inadequate funding for schools in marginalized communities, racial segregation in educational institutions, and implicit biases in the education system contribute to disparities in educational opportunities. Unequal access to education can disadvantage minority individuals, impacting their ability to acquire the knowledge, skills, and credentials necessary for leadership roles.

Training programs and professional development opportunities are essential for building the skills and competencies needed for leadership positions. However, minority leaders often face challenges in accessing these programs. Limited financial resources, lack of awareness about available opportunities, and bias in the selection processes can prevent minority individuals from participating in training and development initiatives. Access to these resources is necessary for them to acquire the required skills and competencies to excel in leadership roles.

Mentorship and guidance from experienced professionals are crucial for career development and advancement. However, minority individuals often have limited access to mentors who share their backgrounds and experiences. This lack of representation in mentorship relationships can make it challenging for minority leaders to find guidance and support from individuals who understand their unique challenges. Without access to mentors who can provide valuable insights, advice, and advocacy, minority leaders may have limited opportunities to navigate their career paths effectively.

Funding and financial resources also play a significant role in career advancement. Scholarships, grants, and funding opportunities can alleviate financial barriers and provide resources for minority individuals to pursue higher education, attend conferences, or engage in leadership development programs. However, unequal access to funding sources and limited financial support can hinder the participation of minority leaders in these opportunities, further perpetuating the underrepresentation of diverse voices in leadership positions.

Addressing unequal access to resources and opportunities requires proactive efforts from organizations, institutions, and communities. It involves creating equitable policies and practices that ensure fair distribution of resources, removing financial barriers through scholarships and financial aid programs, and promoting inclusive training and mentorship initiatives. It also requires organizations to actively seek out and support talented individuals from underrepresented backgrounds, providing them with the necessary resources and opportunities to thrive.

Furthermore, partnerships between educational institutions, community organizations, and industry can help bridge the gap in access to resources and opportunities. Collaborative initiatives can provide mentorship, internships, and networking opportunities that expose minority leaders to diverse experiences and career pathways. By expanding access to resources and opportunities, organizations can foster a more inclusive and diverse leadership pipeline, breaking down systemic barriers and promoting equitable representation of minority leaders.

Removing barriers enabling unequal access to resources and opportunities is essential for advancing diversity, equity, and inclusion in leadership positions. By dismantling barriers and providing equal access to the resources required for career development and advancement, organizations can create a more level playing field, enabling minority leaders to thrive and contribute their unique perspectives and talents to leadership roles.

Organizational Culture and Bias: Organizational culture plays a crucial role in shaping the experiences and opportunities available to minority leaders. A culture that fails to recognize and value diversity can create hostile environments where minority leaders face bias, discrimination, and limited options for growth.

One aspect of organizational culture that can impede the progress of minority leaders is the presence of bias. Bias can be overt or subtle and manifest in various forms, including racial discrimination, gender bias, and bias based on other identities. Biased attitudes and behaviors within an organization can result in exclusion, marginalization, and unequal treatment of minority leaders. These practices undermine their sense of belonging and well-being and restrict their access to resources, mentorship, and career advancement opportunities.

Whether intentional or unintentional, discrimination can also be a significant barrier for minority leaders. Discriminatory practices such as unfair promotion processes, biased performance evaluations, and unequal distribution of resources can perpetuate inequities and hinder the progress of talented minority individuals. Discrimination erodes trust, damages morale, and contributes to a culture of exclusion, where minority leaders become neglected, undervalued, or subjected to systemic barriers that impede their career advancement.

The failure to address these cultural barriers within an organization limits the full potential of minority leaders. When diverse perspectives and experiences are not recognized and valued, organizations miss out on the benefits of diversity, such as innovative ideas, creativity, and different approaches to problem-solving. Homogeneous leadership landscapes lack representation and limit organizations' ability to effectively navigate complex and diverse environments.

An inclusive culture that values and celebrates diversity must cultivate a mindset seeking to overcome bias within its existing organizational environment. Prerequisites include establishing clear policies and practices that promote equity, diversity, and inclusion throughout the organization. It also requires ongoing education and training to raise awareness about bias, discrimination, and the importance of inclusive leadership. Organizations can implement unconscious bias training, diversity and inclusion workshops, and cultural competency programs to address bias and foster a more inclusive environment.

Inclusive leadership practices are also vital for creating a culture that supports the success of minority leaders. Inclusive leaders actively seek diverse perspectives, champion equity and fairness, and create opportunities for underrepresented individuals to contribute and thrive. They foster an environment where all employees feel valued, respected, and empowered to reach their full potential.

Diversifying leadership teams is another critical step in creating an inclusive organizational culture. By actively recruiting and promoting individuals from diverse backgrounds, organizations can challenge the status quo and bring new perspectives and experiences to leadership positions. Having culturally diverse leaders at all levels sends a powerful message that diversity is valued and creates a more inclusive environment for all employees.

Organizations must also be responsive to feedback and willing to address issues of bias and discrimination promptly and effectively. Organizations may need to implement robust reporting mechanisms, conduct thorough investigations, and take appropriate action to address instances of bias or discrimination. By creating a culture of accountability, organizations can foster a safe and inclusive environment where minority leaders can thrive.

Overall, addressing organizational culture and bias is crucial for breaking down systemic barriers and creating inclusive environments that support the success and advancement of minority leaders. It requires a collective effort from organizational leaders, employees, and stakeholders to challenge biases, dismantle discriminatory practices, and foster cultures that embrace diversity, equity, and inclusion.

Addressing these systemic barriers requires intentional efforts from organizations, leaders, and other stakeholders. It involves implementing inclusive policies and practices, fostering diverse representation, challenging biases, and creating equitable opportunities for all individuals to thrive and contribute their unique perspectives and talents. By dismantling these barriers, organizations can unlock the full potential of minority leaders and cultivate inclusive leadership cultures that drive innovation, creativity, and sustainable success.

Creating Inclusive and Supportive Organizational Cultures

Navigating organizational challenges to create inclusive and supportive corporate cultures requires a thoughtful and proactive approach. Here are four ways to navigate these challenges:

Promoting Leadership Commitment: Leadership commitment is crucial for creating an inclusive and supportive organizational culture. Leaders play a pivotal role in shaping an organization's values, norms, and behaviors. Leaders must articulate a clear vision for diversity, equity, and inclusion in promoting leadership commitment. This vision should outline the importance of creating an environment where all individuals feel valued, respected, and included. By clearly communicating this vision, leaders can set expectations and guide the organization's efforts toward inclusivity.

In addition to articulating a vision, leaders must demonstrate their commitment through their actions and decisions, including advocating for diversity initiatives and allocating resources to support diversity efforts. Leaders should actively participate in and champion diversity and inclusion programs, measures, and events within the organization. By actively engaging in these activities, leaders show their commitment and foster a sense of trust and credibility among employees.

Leaders must also hold themselves and others accountable for creating an inclusive environment. Establishing clear goals and objectives and regularly monitoring progress allows leaders to develop systems for feedback and assessment, ensuring the successful integration of diversity and inclusion into performance evaluations and recognition programs. By holding themselves and others accountable, leaders send a strong message that diversity and inclusion are not just empty rhetoric but core values expected to be upheld throughout the organization.

Fostering Employee Engagement: Employee engagement is essential for creating an inclusive and supportive organizational culture. Employees are the lifeblood of an organization, and their perspectives and experiences are invaluable in shaping an inclusive environment. Organizations seeking to foster employee engagement must realize that it is crucial to encourage open dialogue and create spaces where employees feel comfortable sharing their thoughts, ideas, and concerns. Creating open environments begins with establishing regular communication channels, such as team meetings, town halls, or feedback sessions, where employees communicate their perspectives on diversity and inclusion.

Actively seeking employee input in decision-making processes, particularly those that impact diversity and inclusion, is another effective way to foster employee engagement. By involving employees in developing policies, practices, and programs, organizations show that their voices are valued and considered. This sense of ownership and inclusivity can significantly impact employee morale and motivation, as they feel a sense of investment in creating a more inclusive culture.

Furthermore, providing employee resource groups or affinity network opportunities can significantly enhance employee engagement. These groups create spaces for employees with shared experiences or identities to connect, share their experiences, and collaborate on diversity and inclusion initiatives. Employee resource groups can be formed based on various dimensions of diversity, such as race, gender, ethnicity, or LGBTQ+

identities. By fostering these communities, organizations empower employees to drive change and provide a platform for amplification of their voices within the organization. These groups can also contribute valuable insights and ideas for creating a more inclusive culture and help organizations address different employee communities' specific needs and challenges.

Implementing Bias Training: Implementing bias training and education programs is crucial in creating an inclusive and supportive organizational culture. These programs help employees recognize their implicit biases and provide them with strategies for mitigating the influence of biases on their decision-making processes. The training should build empathy and cultural competence, helping employees understand the perspectives and experiences of individuals from diverse backgrounds. Organizations can promote more inclusive behaviors and decision-making practices by increasing awareness of biases.

In addition to addressing biases, it is vital to provide education on the value of diversity and inclusion. Instruction includes sharing the business case for diversity, highlighting how a diverse workforce contributes to innovation, problem-solving, and organizational success. Organizations can foster a culture that values and appreciates diverse perspectives, experiences, and talents by giving employees a deeper understanding of the benefits of diversity and inclusion. Education on diversity and inclusion can also help dispel myths and misconceptions, promoting a more inclusive and supportive work environment.

Implementing practical bias training and education programs requires organizations to ensure they are ongoing and integrated into the organizational culture. Offering regular refresher sessions and providing opportunities for continuous learning and growth ensures the consistent reinforcement and application of knowledge and skills acquired through training. By integrating bias training and education as a core component of professional development, organizations can embed inclusive practices into their daily operations and foster a culture that actively challenges biases and promotes equitable decision-making.

Establishing Inclusive Policies and Practices: Establishing inclusive policies and practices is a fundamental step in creating an inclusive and supportive organizational culture. It involves reviewing and revising existing policies and procedures to ensure they promote diversity, equity, and inclusion at all levels of the organization. These reviews include examining hiring practices to ensure that diverse candidate pools remain active and that there is a commitment to equal opportunity. By actively seeking out and attracting candidates from diverse backgrounds, organizations can increase the likelihood of hiring individuals who bring diverse perspectives and experiences to the workforce.

Creating transparent promotion and performance evaluation processes is another important aspect of establishing inclusive policies and practices. Organizations should ensure clear criteria and standards for career advancement and that they are applied consistently and fairly across all employees. By eliminating bias and favoritism from the promotion process, organizations create a level playing field where individuals are evaluated based on their skills, qualifications, and potential rather than their demographic characteristics.

Establishing mentorship and sponsorship programs is also critical for supporting the career development of minority employees. These programs pair minority employees with experienced leaders who can provide guidance, support, and advocacy. Mentors and sponsors can help navigate the complexities of the workplace, offer career advice, and provide networking opportunities. By creating structured mentoring programs, organizations can facilitate the growth and advancement of minority employees and help them overcome possible barriers.

Regularly reviewing policies and practices is essential to identify and address any biases or barriers within the organization. Reviews include conducting regular diversity audits, analyzing workforce demographics, and soliciting employee feedback. By actively seeking input and feedback, organizations can identify areas for improvement and make necessary adjustments to ensure that policies and practices align with their commitment to diversity, equity, and inclusion. Ongoing monitoring and evaluation of these policies and procedures are central to ensuring their effectiveness and creating a culture of continuous improvement.

These four strategies are not exhaustive, and organizations may need to tailor their approach to specific contexts and challenges. Creating an inclusive and supportive organizational culture requires ongoing commitment, continuous learning, and adaptability. Regularly assess progress, gather feedback, and make necessary adjustments to ensure the organization remains on track toward creating an inclusive and supportive environment for all employees. An increase in opportunity for positive organizational change occurs when open and transparent conversations about diversity policies and practices within an organization become the norm and a genuine staple of its core values.

Promoting Leadership Diversity Within Government

Promoting leadership diversity within government organizations is crucial for ensuring inclusive and representative governance. By actively seeking to diversify leadership positions, governments can tap into a broader range of perspectives and experiences, better reflect the diversity of their populations, and make more informed and equitable decisions. Here are six key strategies and real examples of initiatives aimed at promoting leadership diversity in government organizations:

Implementing Diversity and Inclusion Initiatives Within Government Organizations: Implementing diversity and inclusion initiatives within government organizations is a powerful and influential strategy for promoting leadership diversity. These initiatives involve creating policies and programs prioritizing representation and providing opportunities for underrepresented groups to enter and advance in leadership positions. By acknowledging the importance of diversity and inclusion, governments can foster a more inclusive and equitable workplace culture.

The Federal Diversity and Inclusion Excellence Award in the United States exemplifies such an initiative. This award recognizes federal agencies that demonstrate excellence in diversity and inclusion efforts. It encourages agencies to develop strategies and implement practices that promote diversity at all levels of leadership. This initiative encourages other government organizations to follow suit and adopt similar practices by recognizing and highlighting agencies that prioritize diversity and inclusion.

Diversity and inclusion initiatives can include a range of strategies, such as targeted recruitment efforts, training programs to address biases, mentoring and sponsorship programs for underrepresented groups, and creating inclusive policies and practices. These initiatives aim to remove barriers and create a supportive environment for individuals from diverse backgrounds to succeed in leadership roles.

By implementing comprehensive diversity and inclusion initiatives, governments send a clear message that diversity is valued and necessary for effective governance. These initiatives help attract and retain talented individuals from underrepresented groups, ensuring that leadership positions reflect the diversity of the population they serve. Diversity and inclusion initiatives also contribute to improved decision-making processes by incorporating diverse perspectives, experiences, and ideas into policy development and implementation.

Affirmative Action Policies and Quota Systems: Affirmative action policies and quota systems are practical tools governments can use to promote leadership diversity. These policies address historical disadvantages and promote equitable representation of marginalized groups in government organizations. India provides a notable example of such policies with its reservation quotas for Scheduled Castes, Scheduled Tribes, and Other Backward Classes in government jobs and political offices.

The reservation quotas in India are enshrined in the Constitution and have been in place since the country's independence. These quotas allocate a certain percentage of seats and positions in government institutions and elected bodies to individuals from marginalized communities. The purpose of these quotas is to provide opportunities and representation for historically disadvantaged groups, ensuring their participation in decision-making processes.

The impact of affirmative action policies and quota systems can be significant. They provide a pathway for individuals from marginalized backgrounds to access leadership positions that may have been historically inaccessible to them. These policies contribute to diversifying leadership and decision-making processes by addressing systemic barriers and creating opportunities.

However, it's important to note that the impact of affirmative action policies can vary depending on the context and implementation. Critics argue that these policies can lead to reverse discrimination or undermine meritocracy. Ongoing debates exist about the appropriate balance between promoting diversity and ensuring equal opportunities based on merit. Striking the right balance requires careful consideration and periodic evaluation of the effectiveness and fairness of these policies.

As for the potential impact of the 2023 Supreme Court ruling on affirmative action, it is challenging to provide an analysis of its implications since the ruling was released shortly before completing this book. However, the impact of any Supreme Court ruling on affirmative action will depend on the specific provisions and scope of the ruling. Supreme Court decisions can shape the legal landscape and influence government policies related to affirmative action.

It's worth noting that the interpretation and implementation of affirmative action policies can evolve as societal perspectives and legal frameworks change. Governments must monitor and adapt their policies to align with changing notions of fairness, equity, and inclusivity.

In summary, governments can promote leadership diversity through affirmative action policies and quota systems that aim to provide equitable representation for marginalized groups. Examples such as India's reservation quotas demonstrate the potential impact of such policies in creating opportunities and breaking down systemic barriers. However, the effectiveness and fairness of these policies require careful evaluation and consideration. Any potential impact of the 2023 Supreme Court ruling on affirmative action will depend on the specific details of the ruling and its subsequent interpretation and implementation.

Leadership Development Programs (LDPs): Leadership development programs tailored to underrepresented groups are essential to promoting leadership diversity within government organizations. These programs recognize individuals' unique challenges from marginalized backgrounds and provide targeted support to help them develop their leadership potential. The United Kingdom's Civil Service Fast Stream program is an exemplary initiative that offers various opportunities to enhance diversity in senior government roles.

One specific program within the Civil Service Fast Stream is the Summer Diversity Internship Program (SDIP). The SDIP focuses on recruiting and supporting individuals from underrepresented groups, such as ethnic minorities, people with disabilities, and individuals from low socioeconomic backgrounds. The program provides paid internships and valuable work experience in government departments, enabling participants to gain insights into public service and develop leadership skills.

Through the SDIP, participants receive mentorship and guidance from experienced civil servants who provide support throughout their internship. This mentorship fosters a supportive environment that helps underrepresented individuals navigate the complexities of government work and build valuable networks. The program also offers training and development opportunities to enhance participants' skills and competencies, preparing them for future leadership positions.

The Summer Diversity Internship Program significantly impacts leadership diversity within the UK government. The program aims to address the existing disparities and ensure equal access to leadership roles by explicitly targeting underrepresented groups. By providing these opportunities, the program helps break down barriers and challenges faced by underrepresented individuals, empowering them to pursue careers in government and contribute to policy-making processes.

Leadership development programs like the Summer Diversity Internship Program are vital in cultivating a diverse and inclusive leadership pipeline within government organizations. By providing targeted support, mentorship, and networking opportunities, these programs help underrepresented individuals overcome barriers and gain the skills and experiences necessary for leadership roles. Such initiatives contribute to a more representative and effective government that can better address the needs and concerns of diverse communities.

Transparent and Merit-Based Recruitment: Transparent and merit-based recruitment processes are crucial for promoting leadership diversity within government organizations. By implementing practices that remove personal identifiers and focus solely on qualifications, governments can mitigate biases and ensure equal opportunities for all candidates. The Victorian Public Service (VPS) in Australia is an example of an organization that has successfully implemented blind recruitment strategies to increase diversity and combat bias.

The VPS has embraced blind recruitment to address unconscious biases that can influence hiring decisions. Through blind recruitment, personal identifiers such as names, gender, and ethnic background are removed from applications, ensuring that candidates receive evaluations solely based on their skills, qualifications, and experience. This approach helps to level the playing field and promotes fair consideration of candidates from diverse backgrounds.

By adopting blind recruitment practices, the VPS has sought to increase diversity in its workforce. The organization recognizes that by removing unconscious biases, it can attract and hire individuals who may have otherwise faced barriers due to their gender, ethnicity, or other personal characteristics. This commitment to diversity in leadership roles enables the VPS to tap into a broader range of perspectives and experiences, leading to more effective decision-making and improved outcomes for its community.

The implementation of blind recruitment practices by the VPS has demonstrated positive results. The organization has seen an increase in the representation of women, people from culturally diverse backgrounds, and individuals with disabilities in its workforce. This increase in diversity not only enhances the VPS's ability to address the needs of a diverse population but also creates an inclusive and equitable work environment where all employees can thrive and contribute effectively.

Blind recruitment is not a standalone solution but a valuable step toward promoting inclusive leadership within government organizations. To create a comprehensive approach, it complements other diversity and inclusion initiatives, such as targeted outreach and mentorship programs. By ensuring transparency, fairness, and merit-based evaluation, governments can attract a diverse talent pool and provide opportunities for individuals from underrepresented groups to contribute their skills and expertise in leadership roles.

The success of blind recruitment strategies in organizations like the VPS underscores the importance of adopting fair and inclusive practices in recruitment processes. By removing personal identifiers and focusing on merit, governments can foster a more diverse and representative leadership cadre that reflects the diversity of the communities they serve.

Collaboration with External Organizations: Collaboration with external organizations is a valuable strategy for governments to promote leadership diversity. By partnering with organizations specializing in diversity and inclusion, governments can tap into their expertise, resources, and networks to identify talented individuals and support their development. The White House Initiative on Asian Americans and Pacific Islanders (WHIAAPI) in the United States is an example of a government initiative that collaborates with external organizations to advance the inclusion of Asian Americans and Pacific Islanders in leadership roles.

The WHIAAPI works to promote the interests of Asian Americans and Pacific Islanders by engaging with community organizations, stakeholders, and policymakers. The initiative can leverage its knowledge and reach to identify potential leaders from underrepresented communities through partnerships with external organizations. These partnerships help create pathways for talented individuals to access leadership opportunities within government organizations.

Collaboration with external organizations also provides governments with valuable insights and perspectives that can inform the development of inclusive policies. Governments and external organizations can identify systemic barriers and develop strategies to overcome them by working together. This collaborative approach ensures that policies and initiatives are tailored to the needs and experiences of diverse communities, ultimately leading to more effective and impactful outcomes.

External organizations can also be critical in providing resources and support for leadership development programs. They may offer mentorship programs, training opportunities, and networking events targeting underrepresented groups. Through collaboration, governments can leverage these resources to enhance their leadership development initiatives and create a supportive ecosystem that nurtures and empowers aspiring leaders.

The partnership between government initiatives like WHIAAPI and external organizations exemplifies the power of collaboration in driving leadership diversity. By joining forces, governments and external organizations can pool their resources, knowledge, and networks to create a collective impact. Together, they can challenge systemic barriers, advocate for policy changes, and build a more inclusive leadership landscape that reflects the diversity of their societies.

In summary, collaboration with external organizations is an effective strategy for governments to promote leadership diversity. By partnering with organizations focusing on diversity and inclusion, governments can tap into their expertise, resources, and networks to identify talent, develop inclusive policies, and support leadership development programs. Through collaboration, governments can create pathways for underrepresented groups to access leadership opportunities and foster an inclusive and equitable society.

Leadership Accountability and Reporting: Leadership accountability and reporting are essential to promoting diversity and inclusion within government organizations. By integrating diversity targets and reporting mechanisms into performance evaluations, governments can ensure that leaders actively work towards creating an inclusive environment and advancing diversity goals.

One identifiable example of this approach is the Australian Public Service (APS) Commission, which mandates agencies to report on their workforce diversity and inclusion outcomes annually. This reporting requirement serves multiple purposes. Firstly, it promotes transparency by making agencies accountable for their diversity efforts. By publicly disclosing their progress, agencies are held to a higher standard and are more likely to prioritize diversity and inclusion in their leadership practices.

Secondly, reporting on diversity outcomes provides governments with valuable data to assess the effectiveness of their diversity initiatives. It allows them to identify areas of improvement and develop targeted strategies to address gaps or challenges. This data-driven approach helps governments make informed decisions and continuously improve their efforts to promote diversity and inclusion within their organizations.

By including diversity targets in performance evaluations, governments can ensure that leaders actively champion diversity and hold themselves accountable for progress. This accountability fosters a culture of inclusion, where leaders recognize the importance of diversity and actively work towards creating an environment that embraces and values differences.

Furthermore, incorporating diversity targets into performance evaluations sends a strong message to leaders about the importance of diversity and inclusion. It signals that creating an inclusive culture is not just a matter of preference but a strategic imperative for the organization's success. This recognition at the highest levels of leadership can drive meaningful change and encourage leaders to prioritize diversity and inclusion in their decision-making processes.

Regular reporting of diversity outcomes also allows for benchmarking and sharing of best practices across government agencies. It will enable agencies to learn from each other, exchange ideas, and replicate successful strategies. This collaboration and knowledge-sharing contribute to a collective effort to advance diversity and inclusion within the government sector.

Moreover, public reporting on diversity outcomes can have broader societal impacts. It demonstrates the government's commitment to diversity and inclusion, serving as a role model for other organizations. By leading by example, governments can inspire private sector organizations and other institutions to prioritize diversity and implement similar accountability and reporting mechanisms.

Accountability and reporting in leadership diversity also help build public trust and confidence in government organizations. Governments can enhance their legitimacy and credibility by demonstrating their commitment to creating a diverse and inclusive workforce. This transparency can foster stronger relationships between government organizations and their communities, leading to more effective governance and better outcomes.

In conclusion, leadership accountability and reporting are crucial in promoting diversity and inclusion within government organizations. By integrating diversity targets into performance evaluations and requiring regular reporting on diversity outcomes, governments can foster transparency, hold leaders accountable, drive continuous improvement, and inspire broader societal change. These mechanisms help create a culture of inclusion, enhance public trust, and contribute to the overall success of government organizations in building diverse and equitable societies.

By implementing these strategies and learning from real examples of initiatives, governments can foster leadership diversity and create more inclusive and representative public institutions. Promoting diversity within government organizations is not only a matter of equity and social justice but also enhances decision-making, increases public trust, and strengthens democracy by ensuring that diverse voices are heard and considered in developing and implementing policies and programs.

Questions for Leadership Discussion

1. How can leadership development programs tailored to underrepresented groups effectively enhance their leadership skills and empower them to pursue senior roles? Are there any successful examples of such programs from different countries that we can learn from?

2. In what ways can blind recruitment practices contribute to fairer and more inclusive recruitment processes in my/our organization? What challenges might arise when implementing these practices, and how can they be overcome?

3. How can collaborations with external organizations and networks focused on diversity and inclusion support us in identifying talent and developing inclusive policies? What are some potential barriers to effective collaboration, and how can we ensure that these partnerships are mutually beneficial?

4. What are some specific diversity targets that can be included in performance evaluations to hold government leaders accountable for promoting diversity and inclusion? How can governments ensure that these targets are ambitious yet achievable?

5. How might the 2023 Supreme Court ruling on affirmative action impact my/our organization's approach to diversity initiatives? What lessons can be drawn from international examples of affirmative action and quota systems to inform policies in our country?

CHAPTER EIGHT

Allies and Advocates: Driving Change Together

> *The value of allies and advocates in minority leadership lies in their commitment to promoting equity, their ability to influence change, and their dedication to fostering an inclusive culture where all individuals have equal opportunities to thrive and contribute their talents.*

The significance of forging alliances across various backgrounds, experiences, and perspectives cannot be overstated in a world where diversity, equity, and inclusion have become paramount. Let's explore the fundamental principles of allyship and advocacy, showcasing inspiring stories of individuals and organizations collaborating to break down barriers, dismantle systemic biases, and foster a more inclusive and equitable society. Additionally, we'll delve into the transformative power of collective action and the pivotal roles allies, and advocates play in creating positive change.

By understanding the unique challenges faced by minority leaders and underrepresented groups, allies become catalysts for change, working alongside advocates to amplify voices, challenge discrimination, and champion equal opportunities. It is vital to explore how advocacy initiatives, both at the grassroots and organizational levels, have shaped social progress and policy reform. Together, as allies and advocates, we can collectively drive change, shaping a brighter and more harmonious future for all, where diversity is celebrated, inclusion is cherished, and every individual is empowered to contribute their full potential to the betterment of society.

The Value of Allies and Advocates in Minority Leadership

Allies and advocates are crucial in advancing minority leadership by amplifying diverse voices, supporting underrepresented individuals, and advocating for inclusive policies and practices. They are individuals from majority or privileged groups who actively use their influence and privilege to stand alongside and support minorities. Allies and advocates can help create a more inclusive environment by challenging biases and stereotypes, calling out discriminatory behaviors, and promoting diversity and equity within their spheres of influence.

One significant value of allies and advocates is their ability to serve as bridges between minority leaders and decision-makers. Often, minority leaders may face challenges in having their voices heard and their ideas taken seriously in predominantly homogenous environments. Allies and advocates can use their positions of power and influence to leverage the opinions and perspectives of minority leaders, ensuring that their contributions are acknowledged and that culturally diverse voices are represented in meaningful discussions and decisions.

Furthermore, allies and advocates can help break down systemic barriers that hinder the progress of minority leaders. Using their influence to promote equitable policies and practices, they create a level playing field for all individuals, regardless of their background. The most likely result is a more inclusive organizational culture that fosters the growth and success of minority leaders while also benefitting the organization through diverse perspectives and innovative ideas. Ultimately, allies and advocates act as catalysts for change, supporting and championing minority leaders in their journey toward success and creating a more equitable and inclusive society.

In addition to promoting diversity and inclusion, allies and advocates help build a sense of belonging and psychological safety for minority leaders. By publicly expressing support and standing up against discrimination, they create an environment where individuals from diverse backgrounds feel welcomed and valued. This sense of belonging is essential for empowering minority leaders to bring their authentic selves to their roles, fostering creativity, and contributing their unique perspectives to drive positive change.

Moreover, allies and advocates can play a role in educating others within their communities about the importance of diversity and inclusion. They can engage in conversations and workshops to raise awareness about the challenges faced by minority leaders and the benefits of embracing diversity. Through education and advocacy, they can encourage their peers and colleagues to actively support underrepresented individuals, cultivating a broader support network for minority leaders.

Ultimately, the value of allies and advocates in minority leadership lies in their commitment to promoting equity, their ability to influence change, and their dedication to fostering an inclusive culture where all individuals have equal opportunities to thrive and contribute their talents. Their actions, whether big or small, significantly impact breaking down barriers, creating more inclusive spaces, and paving the way for a future where diverse voices are genuinely heard and celebrated in leadership roles.

Practical Tips for Backing and Amplifying Minority Voices

Active Listening and Validation: Active listening and validation are essential to creating an inclusive and supportive environment for minority voices. Active listening goes beyond simply hearing someone's words; it involves being fully present and attentive to what the person is saying verbally and non-verbally. This means maintaining eye contact, nodding in acknowledgment, and providing verbal cues (such as "I understand," "Tell me more," or "That must have been challenging") to show that you are engaged in the conversation.

By actively listening to minority voices, you demonstrate that their perspectives are valued and respected. Many individuals from minority groups may have experienced being ignored or overlooked, so genuine and active listening can be a powerful way to counteract that and make them feel seen and heard. Moreover, active listening allows you to understand their experiences, challenges, and perspectives, helping you develop greater empathy and cultural competence.

Validation is equally crucial as it acknowledges the legitimacy of their experiences and emotions. When you validate someone's feelings, you are not necessarily agreeing with everything they say but instead showing empathy and respect for their point of view. Validating their experiences helps build trust and rapport, creating a safe space for open dialogue and sharing.

For instance, if a minority colleague shares an experience of discrimination or bias, validating their feelings might involve responding with statements like, "I'm sorry you had to go through that," or "Understandably, you feel upset about this situation." Doing so demonstrates that you believe their experiences are real and worthy of consideration.

Active listening and validation can lead to more inclusive decision-making processes in professional settings. When individual voices feel heard and respected, they are more likely to openly contribute their ideas and perspectives, leading to a more diverse range of viewpoints and better-informed decisions. Additionally, active listening and validation can foster a sense of belonging and psychological safety, encouraging minority individuals to actively participate in team discussions and share their unique insights and expertise.

Active listening and validation are powerful tools for backing and amplifying minority voices. They promote a culture of empathy, openness, and inclusivity, laying the foundation for a diverse and thriving organization where everyone's contributions are recognized and valued.

Be An Ally In Meetings: Being an ally in meetings is a proactive way to support and uplift minority voices, fostering an inclusive and equitable environment. When you observe that a minority colleague's input is not acknowledged or overshadowed, stepping in as an ally can help to correct this imbalance and ensure that their ideas receive the attention they deserve. One essential aspect of being an ally in meetings is listening for moments when a minority colleague tries to contribute but does not have the space or opportunity to do so. In such situations, you can tactfully intervene and redirect the conversation to their idea or give them a chance to speak.

Being an ally also involves acknowledging and attributing ideas appropriately. When a minority colleague shares a valuable insight or suggestion, credit them explicitly for their contribution. These actions recognize their input and reinforce the message that diverse perspectives are vital to the team's success. By doing so, you show genuine support for minority voices and create a culture where everyone's ideas are acknowledged, regardless of their background or identity.

It is crucial to be an ally consistently, not just in isolated incidents. In other words, being vigilant and proactive in every meeting ensures that minority voices maintain relevance, respect, and amplification. Cultivate a mindset that actively seeks diverse perspectives and encourages open dialogue among all team members.

Additionally, you must be aware of your privilege and biases as an ally. Understand that your voice may carry more weight or be more readily accepted in specific settings and use that privilege to create opportunities for others to have their voices heard. Be mindful of any unconscious biases that might influence your interactions with minority colleagues and work to overcome them.

Being an ally in meetings contributes to a workplace culture where all team members feel valued and included and where diverse ideas are celebrated and embraced. This kind of supportive environment not only enhances team dynamics but also leads to more innovative solutions and better decision-making. As allies, individuals can collectively create positive change and promote a more inclusive and equitable workplace for everyone.

Creating Opportunities for Visibility: Creating opportunities for visibility is a powerful way to back and amplify minority voices in the workplace. Many talented individuals, especially from underrepresented groups, may not receive the recognition they deserve due to systemic barriers or lack of opportunities. As a proactive measure, organizations can take intentional steps to showcase the expertise and contributions of minority employees. Here's how:

1. **Conference Speaking Engagements:** Actively encourage and support minority employees to speak at internal and

external conferences. Conferences are excellent platforms for knowledge-sharing and networking, and having diverse voices as speakers enriches the event and provides fresh perspectives. Organizations can help minority employees prepare for speaking engagements by offering training or mentoring to boost their confidence and presentation skills.

2. **Panel Discussions:** Involve minority employees in panel discussions on topics related to their expertise. Panels are great opportunities for individuals to share their insights, engage in meaningful conversations, and establish recognition as subject matter experts. Including diverse voices on panels enhances the diversity of thought presented and enriches the overall experience for the audience.

3. **Leadership of Important Projects:** Empower minority employees by giving them leadership opportunities on high-impact projects. Assigning them roles where their skills shine and their leadership qualities are evident benefits the projects and demonstrate to the organization that they are trusted, valued, and capable leaders.

4. **Employee Spotlights and Awards:** Establish employee spotlight features or awards that recognize outstanding contributions from diverse employees. Highlighting their achievements through company-wide communications, newsletters, or social media platforms boosts their visibility and shows the organization's commitment to diversity and inclusion.

5. **Mentorship and Sponsorship Programs:** Implement mentorship and sponsorship programs where minority employees can access senior leaders who can advocate for their advancement. Sponsors can use their influence to create opportunities for their mentees to present their ideas or take on challenging assignments, further enhancing visibility.

6. **Internal Forums and Webinars**: Organize internal forums and webinars where employees can share their expertise and experiences with colleagues. These spaces and opportunities foster a culture of learning and collaboration and provide a platform for lesser-heard voices to be heard and acknowledged.

Creating opportunities for visibility goes beyond tokenism; it is about recognizing and appreciating the diverse talent within the organization and ensuring that everyone has a chance to shine. By doing so, organizations can harness the full potential of their workforce, promote a culture of inclusivity, and inspire others to value and celebrate diversity. Additionally, it sends a positive message to current and potential employees that the organization actively supports and nurtures talent from all backgrounds, making it an attractive and inclusive workplace.

Mentorship and Sponsorship: Mentorship and sponsorship are dynamic tools for supporting the career growth and advancement of minority colleagues within the workplace. They are so vital to the development and success of leaders that it is worthy to continue exploring their value. These relationships offer unique benefits and significantly foster a more inclusive and supportive environment. Here's a deeper look at the importance of mentorship and sponsorship:

1. **Personalized Guidance and Support:** Mentorship provides a safe and confidential space for minority employees to seek advice, share concerns, and gain insights from more experienced colleagues. Mentors can offer guidance on career development, skill-building, and navigating organizational challenges. They can help their mentees set goals and develop action plans to achieve them, which can be particularly beneficial for individuals facing unique barriers or obstacles in their career paths.

2. **Building Confidence and Belonging:** For many minority employees, having a mentor or sponsor who is supportive and invested in their success can significantly impact their sense of belonging and confidence within the organization. The guidance and validation from a mentor or sponsor can help combat imposter syndrome and reinforce the belief that they belong and can thrive in leadership roles.

3. **Exposure to New Opportunities:** Sponsors, remarkably, actively advocate for their mentees' career advancement. They use their influence within the organization to ensure deserving individuals receive consideration for high-visibility assignments, promotions, and leadership opportunities. This exposure to new opportunities can be transformative for minority employees, allowing them to showcase their skills and potential to a broader audience.

4. **Expanding Networks:** Both mentors and sponsors can introduce their mentees to valuable networks and connections, which are instrumental in career advancement. By facilitating introductions to influential individuals within and outside the organization, mentors, and sponsors open doors for their mentees that may have otherwise been difficult to access.

5. **Knowledge Transfer and Cultural Understanding**: Mentorship and sponsorship relationships facilitate knowledge transfer regarding professional skills and understanding the organization's culture and unwritten rules. For minority employees, understanding the organizational culture and dynamics is crucial for their success, and mentors and sponsors can provide valuable insights in this regard.

6. **Mutual Learning and Growth:** Mentorship and sponsorship relationships are mutually beneficial. Mentors and sponsors gain from these relationships through exposure to different perspectives and experiences. Engaging with mentees from diverse backgrounds can broaden mentors' understanding of inclusivity issues and help them become more effective allies in promoting diversity and inclusion.

7. **Long-lasting Impact:** Effective mentorship and sponsorship can impact the mentees' careers, opening doors to future opportunities and setting them on a trajectory for success. Moreover, as mentees progress in their careers, they may, in turn, become mentors or

sponsors for other aspiring minority leaders, creating a positive cycle of support and empowerment.

In summary, mentorship and sponsorship are critical elements in fostering an inclusive and supportive organizational culture. These relationships provide much-needed guidance, support, and advocacy for minority employees, helping them overcome barriers and advance in their careers. By investing in mentorship and sponsorship programs, organizations can empower their diverse talent, cultivate a culture of support, and ultimately contribute to developing a more diverse and inclusive leadership landscape.

Educate Yourself: Educating yourself on the challenges faced by minority groups and the significance of diversity and inclusion is essential in becoming an effective ally and advocate. Here are some key reasons why self-education is crucial:

Increased Empathy and Understanding: When you take the time to educate yourself about the experiences and struggles of minority individuals, you gain insights into the adversities they may encounter in their personal and professional lives. Heightened awareness fosters increased empathy as you begin to comprehend the challenges they face daily. Understanding the systemic barriers and discrimination many minorities confront helps you see the world through their eyes, leading to a more compassionate and considerate approach in your interactions with them.

Empathy is crucial in building authentic relationships and fostering a sense of belonging for minority colleagues.

Demonstrating genuine understanding and concern creates a safe space for minorities to share their perspectives, hardships, and aspirations. In turn, it promotes trust and openness, making it more likely for individuals to feel supported and valued within the workplace. Additionally, empathy extends beyond just listening; it motivates action. When you grasp the difficulties faced by minority individuals, you are more inclined to advocate for their needs and work towards creating an inclusive environment where everyone can thrive.

Challenging Unconscious Bias: Challenging unconscious bias is a continuous process that begins with self-awareness and education. By educating yourself about the various forms of bias and how they can manifest in the workplace, you become better equipped to recognize when these biases may influence your thoughts, actions, and decisions. This awareness allows you to pause and critically assess situations, enabling you to make more objective and fair judgments rather than being guided by unconscious stereotypes or prejudices.

Moreover, as you challenge your unconscious biases, you become a role model for others in the organization. Your commitment to self-improvement and growth sends a powerful message about the importance of inclusivity and fairness. It encourages those around you to reflect on their own biases and work towards creating a more equitable workplace for everyone. As more individuals within the organization take active steps to challenge their preconceptions, it creates a collective movement toward a more inclusive and supportive culture where minority voices receive the respect and consideration they deserve. Challenging unconscious bias is not about being perfect or entirely eradicating discrimination but rather about fostering an environment where individuals continuously strive to be more fair, empathetic, and understanding toward one another.

Finally, challenging unconscious bias benefits the workplace and extends to interactions outside of work. As you develop a deeper understanding of unconscious biases and actively work to challenge them, you become more mindful of your behavior and attitudes in various social settings. This mindfulness can positively impact relationships, conversations, and engagements with people from diverse backgrounds.

By promoting empathy, respect, and inclusivity in all aspects of your life, you contribute to the broader societal effort of breaking down systemic barriers and fostering a more equitable and harmonious world. Embracing the journey of challenging unconscious bias not only elevates the voices of minorities in your immediate workplace but also contributes to the larger goal of building a society where everyone is valued and empowered.

Fostering Inclusive Behavior: Fostering inclusive behavior goes beyond acknowledging the importance of diversity and inclusion; it involves taking concrete actions to create an equitable and supportive atmosphere. As you educate yourself on the challenges faced by minority groups, you become more aware of the subtle ways in which exclusion can manifest in everyday interactions. With this heightened awareness, you can proactively work to create an environment where everyone feels welcome and appreciated.

One way to foster inclusive behavior is by actively listening to others and seeking diverse perspectives. When engaging in conversations or decision-making processes, encourage individuals from different backgrounds to share their ideas and thoughts. By valuing and considering culturally diverse viewpoints, you contribute to a culture that embraces the richness of varied experiences and promotes innovative thinking.

Inclusive behavior also involves recognizing and challenging microaggressions and biased language. Be attentive to your words and actions, ensuring they do not perpetuate stereotypes or inadvertently exclude others. Instead, strive to use language that is inclusive, respectful, and affirming of everyone's identities.

Additionally, creating opportunities for collaboration and teamwork can enhance inclusivity within the workplace. Encourage cross-functional projects and diverse teams to work together, fostering an environment where individuals from different backgrounds can contribute their unique skills and insights. By actively promoting cooperation and mutual respect among team members, you continue to create spaces where minority voices are heard and valued for the distinct perspectives they bring to the organization.

Fostering inclusive behavior requires a genuine commitment to understanding and valuing diversity and consistent efforts to translate that understanding into action. It is an ongoing process of self-reflection, learning, and growth, but its positive impact on individuals and the organization is immeasurable. Embracing and promoting inclusivity in your interactions not only empowers minority voices but also contributes to building a stronger, more harmonious, and forward-thinking workplace culture.

Effective Communication: Effective communication is pivotal in promoting organizational diversity and inclusion. You develop the skills to communicate more effectively with colleagues from diverse backgrounds through education and a deeper understanding of diversity-related issues. These skills include actively listening to their experiences, concerns, and perspectives and responding with empathy and respect. By engaging in open and honest conversations about diversity, you create a safe and supportive space where individuals feel comfortable sharing their unique insights and experiences.

Education also equips you with the knowledge to navigate potentially sensitive topics related to diversity and inclusion. You become better equipped to address misconceptions, biases, or conflicts that may arise, and you can do so in a manner that promotes understanding and learning rather than confrontation. This type of communication fosters a culture of inclusivity and encourages others to participate in discussions without fear of judgment or marginalization.

Furthermore, effective communication helps build trust and rapport among colleagues, essential for a cohesive and productive work environment. Employees who feel their voices are heard and respected are more likely to be engaged and motivated. It can lead to increased collaboration and teamwork and improved problem-solving and decision-making processes.

Inclusive communication also extends to how you convey information and ideas. Being mindful of the language and examples used in presentations, emails, or reports can help avoid reinforcing stereotypes or inadvertently excluding certain groups. By using inclusive language and being sensitive to the diverse audience, you create an environment where everyone feels seen, valued, and understood.

Effective communication, driven by education and understanding, is fundamental for promoting diversity and inclusion within the organization. It empowers you to engage in meaningful and respectful conversations about diversity-related topics, creating an atmosphere of openness and acceptance. By embracing inclusive communication practices, you contribute to a workplace culture that celebrates diversity, fosters collaboration, and enables all employees to thrive and reach their full potential.

Identifying Systemic Barriers: Self-education plays a critical role in identifying and understanding systemic barriers that may impede the progress of minority voices within the organization. As you educate yourself on diversity and inclusion issues, you become more aware of the various forms of bias, discrimination, and inequities in workplace structures, policies, and practices. Elevated awareness enables you to recognize the specific challenges faced by minority individuals and groups, including barriers to career advancement, limited access to resources, and unequal growth opportunities.

By identifying systemic barriers, you can then take proactive steps to address and dismantle them. Measures may involve advocating for changes in organizational policies and practices that perpetuate inequality or discrimination. For example, you can support initiatives promoting diverse hiring practices, implement mentorship programs, or provide equitable training and development opportunities. In doing so, you contribute to creating a workplace environment that values and supports all employees, regardless of their background or identity.

Furthermore, self-education allows you to engage in informed conversations with colleagues and decision-makers about the importance of addressing systemic barriers. As you share your knowledge and insights, you can encourage others to recognize and confront these barriers, fostering a collective commitment to creating a more inclusive and supportive workplace culture.

Moreover, being informed about systemic barriers helps you challenge the status quo and push for meaningful changes that can lead to greater diversity and representation in leadership positions. By actively working to break down these barriers, you contribute to a workplace where minority voices are not only heard but also empowered to influence decision-making processes and contribute to the organization's success.

Self-education empowers you to identify and understand the systemic barriers that hinder the progress of minority voices within the workplace. Armed with this knowledge, you can take purposeful action to address these barriers and advocate for meaningful changes that promote diversity, equity, and inclusion. By actively working to dismantle systemic barriers, you contribute to creating a workplace culture that is truly inclusive and supportive of all employees, paving the way for more excellent representation and opportunities for minority individuals to thrive and succeed.

Supporting Inclusive Policies: Supporting inclusive policies is necessary to leverage your self-education to promote diversity and inclusion within your organization. By understanding the significance of diversity and its impact on organizational success, you can effectively advocate for policies prioritizing inclusivity and representation. Armed with knowledge about the benefits of diverse perspectives and experiences, you can present evidence-based arguments to decision-makers, highlighting how inclusive policies can lead to improved innovation, creativity, and problem-solving.

One way to support inclusive policies is by actively participating in discussions and initiatives related to diversity and inclusion. By voicing your support for policies that promote equal opportunities, diverse hiring practices, and mentorship programs, you contribute to creating a more equitable work environment. Your input can help shape policies that address systemic barriers and provide a level playing field for all employees, regardless of their background.

Additionally, you can collaborate with other like-minded individuals and employee resource groups to advocate for change collectively. Engaging in grassroots efforts to promote diversity and inclusion within the organization can have a powerful impact, demonstrating a shared commitment to fostering an inclusive workplace culture. By supporting these efforts, you help build momentum and draw attention to the importance of implementing inclusive policies.

Moreover, your knowledge of diversity and inclusion issues can be valuable in creating educational materials and resources for employees and leaders. Sharing this information empowers others to advocate for inclusive policies and practices. This educational approach can help raise awareness and understanding throughout the organization, fostering a culture that actively embraces diversity and works towards breaking down barriers.

Increasing one's knowledge base on diversity and inclusion equips you with the tools and understanding needed to support inclusive policies within your organization. By actively engaging in discussions, collaborating with others, and sharing your knowledge, you can advocate for meaningful change and contribute to building a workplace culture that values and prioritizes diversity and inclusion. Through your efforts, you can create a more welcoming and supportive environment where all employees have equal opportunities to thrive and contribute their unique perspectives and talents.

Building Solidarity: Building solidarity through self-education is foundational to fostering a positive and inclusive work environment. When you take the initiative to educate yourself about the challenges and experiences faced by marginalized groups, it sends a powerful message of empathy and support. Your commitment to understanding these issues demonstrates your willingness to stand in solidarity with your colleagues from diverse backgrounds, acknowledging their struggles and advocating for their inclusion and equal treatment.

Building solidarity creates a sense of trust and camaraderie among team members, regardless of their identity. When colleagues see that you are genuinely interested in learning about their experiences and perspectives, they are more likely to feel valued and respected within the organization. This sense of trust and respect can lead to stronger working relationships, enhanced collaboration, and increased productivity.

Moreover, building solidarity can lead to a more cohesive and harmonious workplace culture. Employees who feel supported and valued for who they are more likely to be engaged and motivated. This positive work culture can have a ripple effect, inspiring others to be more inclusive and respectful, thereby creating a virtuous cycle of support and unity.

In addition to promoting inclusivity within the workplace, building solidarity can extend beyond the organization. As an advocate for diversity and inclusion, you can collaborate with external groups and communities that advocate for equity and justice. By actively participating in community efforts and amplifying the voices of marginalized groups, you contribute to a broader movement toward social change and equality.

Building solidarity through self-education is a powerful way to create a supportive and inclusive work environment. By showing your commitment to understanding and supporting colleagues from diverse backgrounds, you foster trust, respect, and camaraderie within the organization. Results enhance teamwork and productivity and contribute to a more cohesive and harmonious workplace culture. Furthermore, your advocacy for inclusivity can extend beyond the workplace, empowering you to participate in broader social efforts to promote equity and justice.

Being a Role Model: A role model is an effective way to influence positive organizational change. When you prioritize self-education and demonstrate inclusive behaviors, you set a clear example for others. Colleagues and peers notice your commitment to learning about diversity and inclusion issues and genuine efforts to create an inclusive work environment. Your actions can inspire them to become more proactive in seeking knowledge, understanding the experiences of marginalized groups, and promoting inclusivity in their interactions.

As a role model, your behavior catalyzes cultural transformation within the organization. When others see your active engagement in self-education and your willingness to challenge biases and stereotypes, it sends a message that diversity and inclusion are not just buzzwords but core values that should guide the organization's practices. By being consistent in your actions and words, you build credibility and trust, making it more likely for others to join you in advocating for an inclusive workplace culture.

Moreover, being a role model can have a positive impact beyond your immediate circle of colleagues. As others observe your commitment to diversity and inclusion, they may start emulating your behaviors, creating a ripple effect that spreads throughout the organization. Consequently, this may lead to an active cultural shift where inclusivity becomes a shared responsibility and a collective effort to create a more equitable and supportive workplace for all.

Furthermore, being a role model in promoting diversity and inclusion can enhance your leadership capabilities. When you actively prioritize self-education and inclusive behaviors, it showcases your ability to understand and navigate diversity-related issues. As a result, increased respect and recognition from your peers, superiors, and subordinates may present additional opportunities for you to influence positive change at higher levels of the organization.

Being a role model by prioritizing self-education and exhibiting inclusive behaviors is a powerful way to inspire positive organizational change. Your actions serve as a model for others to follow, encouraging them to seek knowledge, challenge biases, and actively support diversity and inclusion efforts. By being consistent in your commitment to inclusivity, you can influence cultural transformation, where diversity and inclusion become integral parts of the organization's identity and practices. Additionally, being a role model can enhance your leadership capabilities and open doors for further opportunities to drive positive change within the workplace.

Contributing to Organizational Success: Embracing diversity and fostering an inclusive environment is a moral imperative and a strategic advantage for organizations. When you prioritize self-education on diversity and inclusion issues and actively promote these principles, you contribute to the organization's success in several ways.

Firstly, diverse teams bring various perspectives, experiences, and skills. Individuals from different backgrounds collaborate and approach problem-solving and decision-making from multiple angles. This diversity of thought leads to more creative and innovative solutions to challenges, giving the organization a competitive edge in the marketplace. By advocating for diversity and inclusion, you help ensure that the organization's talent pool is diverse and that all employees can contribute their unique perspectives and ideas.

Secondly, an inclusive work environment fosters a sense of belonging among employees. When individuals feel valued, respected, and included, they are more likely to be engaged and motivated in their roles. This positive work environment can lead to higher employee satisfaction and retention levels, reducing turnover and the associated costs of recruiting and training new employees. Moreover, a diverse and inclusive workforce is more likely to attract top talent, as individuals gravitate to organizations that prioritize diversity and create a welcoming and supportive workplace culture.

Thirdly, embracing diversity and inclusion can enhance the organization's reputation and brand image. Consumers and stakeholders are increasingly conscious of an organization's commitment to social responsibility and diversity in today's interconnected world. By championing diversity and promoting inclusive practices, the organization can appeal to a broader customer base and build stronger relationships with clients, partners, and communities.

Furthermore, an inclusive culture can lead to improved decision-making processes. When employees from diverse backgrounds have an equal voice in discussions and decision-making, it ensures a more comprehensive and well-rounded analysis of potential options. Better-informed decisions considering a wider range of perspectives and possible outcomes become available.

Again, contributing to organizational success through embracing diversity and fostering an inclusive environment is a matter of ethics and a strategic advantage. By prioritizing self-education on diversity and inclusion issues and actively promoting these principles, you contribute to a more innovative and creative workplace, enhance employee engagement and retention, strengthen the organization's reputation, and improve decision-making processes. Embracing diversity is not just the right thing to do; it's a key driver of success in today's diverse and interconnected world.

Personal Growth: Continuous learning about diversity and inclusion can be a profoundly enriching and transformative experience for personal growth. As you educate yourself on these topics, you become more aware of your biases and assumptions, leading to greater self-reflection and introspection. This process of self-awareness enables you to challenge your preconceived notions and open your mind to different perspectives, ultimately fostering a more empathetic and compassionate outlook.

You expose yourself to diverse voices and experiences by seeking knowledge about diversity and inclusion. This exposure broadens your horizons and helps you appreciate the richness and complexity of human diversity. It encourages you to step outside your comfort zone and converse with individuals from diverse backgrounds, deepening your understanding of their unique struggles, challenges, and triumphs.

Furthermore, learning about diversity and inclusion can equip you with the tools and skills to be a more effective communicator and collaborator. You become more adept at navigating cross-cultural interactions and developing inclusive relationships with colleagues, friends, and community members. This enhanced ability to connect fosters a sense of unity and belonging, creating a more harmonious and supportive social environment.

As you deepen your understanding of diversity and inclusion, you may also discover opportunities for advocacy and activism. The knowledge you gain can inspire you to become a vocal champion for marginalized groups, promoting equitable policies and practices within your organization and society. This sense of purpose and commitment to social justice can be incredibly empowering and fulfilling, contributing to a greater understanding of fulfillment and meaning in your life.

Continually learning about diversity and inclusion is a transformative journey of personal growth. It challenges your beliefs, broadens your perspectives, and enriches your understanding of the world. Through self-awareness and exposure to diverse experiences, you become more empathetic and compassionate, capable of building inclusive relationships and advocating for social justice. This commitment to learning and growth benefits you personally and creates a more diverse, equitable, and inclusive society for everyone.

As we can see, self-education is a powerful tool in becoming an effective ally for minority voices and supporting diversity and inclusion in the workplace. By investing time and effort in learning about the challenges faced by marginalized groups, you can become a more empathetic, informed, and influential advocate for positive change within your organization and beyond.

Questions for leadership discussion

1. How has engaging in continuous learning about diversity and inclusion impacted your personal growth and understanding of the world? Share any specific experiences or realizations that have shaped your perspectives.

2. In what ways has self-education on diversity and inclusion helped you challenge your own biases and assumptions? How have these newfound insights influenced your interactions and relationships with others?

3. Can you describe a situation where your exposure to diverse voices and experiences enriched your understanding of human diversity? How did this experience influence your approach to cross-cultural interactions?

4. Reflecting on your journey of learning about diversity, have you found opportunities for advocacy and activism? How do you envision using your knowledge to promote equitable policies and practices within your organization and community?

5. Share how engaging in conversations and education about diversity has positively influenced your sense of purpose and fulfillment. How do you see yourself contributing to a more inclusive society in the future?

CHAPTER NINE

Overcoming Obstacles: Resilience in the Face of Adversity

Examining the unique challenges of minority leaders goes beyond recognizing broad diversity initiatives. It requires a nuanced understanding of intersectionality, imposter syndrome, cultural intelligence, unconscious biases, networking opportunities, and the expectation of representation.

Understanding the intersectionality of their identities is crucial as minority women, for example, may experience "double jeopardy," encountering both gender and racial discrimination. Imposter syndrome is another significant challenge, where minority leaders fear their success is a result of affirmative action rather than their skills. The lack of cultural intelligence within organizations may lead to exclusionary practices, while unconscious biases and stereotypes can hinder trust and influence. Additionally, the burden of being seen as a token representative and limited networking opportunities further complicate the journey of minority leaders. Examining and addressing these challenges is essential to foster an inclusive environment where they can thrive and contribute fully. This chapter explores the distinctive obstacles faced by minority leaders within organizations.

Examining Unique Challenges of Minority Leaders

Examining the unique challenges of minority leaders requires a comprehensive understanding of the intersectionality of their identities. For instance, minority women may face "double jeopardy" in leadership positions, experiencing gender and racial discrimination simultaneously. This intersectional bias can lead to limited opportunities for advancement and reduced access to resources, posing complex challenges requiring a more nuanced approach.

As mentioned at the beginning of this chapter, another significant challenge faced by minority leaders is the "imposter syndrome." They may internalize feelings of inadequacy or self-doubt, fearing that their success results from affirmative action rather than their skills and qualifications. Overcoming imposter syndrome can be a continuous struggle and may impact their ability to assert themselves confidently in leadership roles.

The absence of cultural intelligence and awareness within organizations can also present unique challenges for minority leaders. Organizational cultures that do not value diversity or are not sensitive to the needs of diverse leaders may result in exclusionary practices and microaggressions. Building cultural competency among colleagues and leadership can foster a more inclusive and supportive environment for minority leaders.

Additionally, minority leaders may face resistance and skepticism from some colleagues who harbor unconscious biases. Stereotypes and preconceived notions about leadership capabilities based on race, ethnicity, or other identities can hinder their gaining trust and influence within the organization. Addressing these biases and fostering open dialogue is essential to overcome such challenges.

Minority leaders may experience the "stereotype threat," where individuals fear confirming negative stereotypes about their racial or ethnic group. This threat can lead to anxiety and undermine their self-confidence in leadership roles. Recognizing and addressing the stereotype threat within the organizational culture is essential for empowering minority leaders to lead authentically and confidently.

Another unique challenge is the burden of being seen as a token representative of their minority group. Minority leaders may feel pressured to conform to certain expectations or be hyper-visible as a representative of diversity in leadership. This burden can detract from their ability to focus on their core responsibilities and personal growth. Creating a more inclusive organizational culture that values diversity and does not place undue expectations on minority leaders is crucial in alleviating this challenge.

Work-life balance is also a significant challenge for minority leaders. As they navigate the complexities of leadership and advocate for diversity, they may find themselves dedicating more time and energy to their roles. Striking a balance between professional and personal commitments can be challenging, and organizations should support minority leaders in maintaining their well-being and overall satisfaction.

Also, the lack of representation at higher leadership levels can hinder the progress of minority leaders. The absence of role models and mentors with similar backgrounds and experiences can make it challenging for aspiring minority leaders to envision their path to success. Organizations must actively work to promote diversity in senior leadership positions, providing more visible role models and mentors to support and guide minority leaders on their leadership journey.

As a result of limited representation at higher levels of leadership, the scarcity of networking opportunities can present itself as another obstacle for minority leaders. Exclusive networks formed through historical power structures may limit their access to influential circles, impacting their ability to secure sponsors and mentors who can advocate for their career advancement. Addressing these networking gaps and creating inclusive opportunities for collaboration is vital for promoting diversity at the leadership level.

Furthermore, minority leaders may face additional scrutiny and pressure to "represent" their communities or address diversity-related issues single-handedly. While they may possess valuable insights, it is essential to recognize that their experiences are not representative of an entire demographic. Organizations must foster collective responsibility for diversity and inclusion rather than burdening individual minority leaders with this task.

Examining the unique challenges of minority leaders goes beyond recognizing broad diversity initiatives. It requires a nuanced understanding of intersectionality, imposter syndrome, cultural intelligence, unconscious biases, networking opportunities, and the expectation of representation. By addressing these challenges and providing targeted support, organizations can create an inclusive and empowering environment that allows minority leaders to thrive and contribute their full potential to the organization's success.

Cultivating Resilience and Emotional Intelligence In Leadership Within An Organization

Cultivating resilience and emotional intelligence is indispensable for effective leadership within an organization. Resilience enables leaders to navigate through adversity, setbacks, and challenges without losing motivation or giving in to stress. Leaders in a constantly changing business environment may face unforeseen circumstances requiring quick decision-making and adaptability. Resilient leaders can stay focused, maintain a positive attitude, and inspire their teams to overcome obstacles and achieve goals. Organizations can foster resilience in their leaders by providing opportunities for training, coaching, and creating a culture that values learning from failures and setbacks as opportunities for growth.

Emotional intelligence (EI) is the ability to recognize, understand, and manage one's emotions and those of others effectively. Leaders with high EI are better equipped to handle conflicts, build strong relationships, and foster a positive work environment. They can empathize with their team members, consider their perspectives, and address their needs and concerns sensitively. Emotionally intelligent leaders are also skilled at giving and receiving feedback constructively, promoting open communication and trust within the organization. Organizations can promote emotional intelligence among their leaders through leadership development programs, emotional intelligence assessments, and fostering a culture that values emotional intelligence as a critical leadership competency.

Effective communication is a critical component of both resilience and emotional intelligence. Leaders who communicate clearly and empathetically are better equipped to navigate challenging situations and build strong team relationships. Transparent communication helps foster trust and transparency, creating a sense of psychological safety within the organization. By encouraging open dialogue and active listening, leaders can better understand the needs and concerns of their team members, which is crucial for cultivating resilience and emotional intelligence.

Self-awareness is another vital aspect of both resilience and emotional intelligence. Self-aware leaders understand their emotions, strengths, and weaknesses, allowing them to manage their reactions and make well-informed decisions. Self-awareness also enables leaders to recognize when they need support and seek help when facing challenges, contributing to their resilience. Organizations can promote self-awareness in leaders through leadership assessments, 360-degree feedback, and regular self-reflection exercises.

Supportive environments prioritizing well-being can significantly contribute to cultivating resilience and emotional intelligence in leaders. Organizations can provide resources such as counseling, stress management workshops, and wellness programs to help leaders cope with stress and maintain their emotional balance. Flexible work arrangements and a culture that values work-life balance also contribute to leaders' emotional well-being, allowing them to lead more clearly and effectively.

Leadership coaching and mentoring can be vital in developing resilience and emotional intelligence. Working with experienced coaches or mentors can help leaders gain insights into their behaviors, emotions, and decision-making processes. Coaches can help leaders identify areas for improvement and develop strategies to enhance their emotional intelligence and resilience. Regular coaching sessions provide a safe space for leaders to explore their emotions, reflect on their leadership style, and receive valuable feedback, ultimately leading to their personal and professional growth as resilient and emotionally intelligent leaders.

Inspiring Stories of Leaders Overcoming Cultural Adversity

Sundar Pichai- CEO of Alphabet Inc.: Sundar Pichai's journey from his humble beginnings in Chennai, India, to becoming the CEO of one of the world's largest technology companies, Alphabet Inc., is a remarkable testament to resilience and determination in the face of cultural adversity. Growing up in a middle-class family in India, Pichai faced significant economic challenges, but his innate curiosity and passion for technology set him apart from an early age. Despite limited resources, he displayed exceptional academic performance and a keen interest in engineering and technology.

Pichai's pursuit of higher education in the United States was challenging. Leaving his home country and adapting to a new cultural environment can be daunting, especially for an international student. However, Pichai's determination to excel and embrace new experiences led him to pursue a Master's in Material Sciences and Engineering from Stanford University. The move to the US required him to navigate cultural differences and the complexities of living far away from home. Still, he persevered, immersing himself in his studies and building a solid foundation for his future career.

His decision to pursue an MBA from the prestigious Wharton School of the University of Pennsylvania further demonstrated his ambition and determination to succeed. During this time, he honed his leadership and management skills, which would later prove invaluable in his rise up the corporate ladder.

Upon joining Google in 2004, Pichai quickly ascended by displaying a unique combination of technical expertise and visionary leadership. He played an important role in developing several groundbreaking products, including Google Chrome, one of the most popular web browsers globally, and Android, the world's most widely used mobile operating system.

Pichai's dedication, intelligence, and strong work ethic did not go unnoticed, and he earned the trust and admiration of Google's co-founders, Larry Page and Sergey Brin. In 2015, he was appointed as the CEO of Google, a significant achievement for a person of a minority background in the tech industry.

In 2019, Pichai's leadership and innovative vision led to another milestone when he was named the CEO of Alphabet Inc., Google's parent company. He oversees various businesses in this role, including Google, Waymo, and other ambitious ventures. Sundar Pichai overcame several challenges throughout his life and career:

Economic Hardships: Pichai was born into a middle-class family in Chennai, India, where financial resources were limited. Despite these economic challenges, he was determined to pursue his passion for technology and education.

Cultural Adaptation: Moving to the United States for higher education meant Pichai had to navigate a new cultural environment and adapt to life far away from his home country. He adjusted to different customs, social norms, and academic systems.

Distance from Family: Leaving his family behind in India to pursue his dreams in the US was emotionally challenging. Being far from home and loved ones can be isolating and daunting, especially for an international student.

Academic Pressure: Pursuing advanced degrees at prestigious institutions like Stanford University and the Wharton School required immense dedication and hard work. Pichai faced academic pressure and the need to excel in competitive educational environments.

Breaking Stereotypes: As a person of Indian origin in the tech industry, Pichai faced stereotypes and biases. Overcoming these prejudices and proving his leadership and innovative capabilities required resilience and determination.

Leadership Challenges: Pichai encountered significant leadership challenges as he rose through the ranks at Google. Leading large teams, making strategic decisions, and managing diverse stakeholders demanded strong leadership skills and the ability to navigate complex corporate landscapes.

High Expectations: Taking on leadership roles at Google and later Alphabet meant Pichai had to meet high expectations as the CEO of one of the most influential companies in the world. The pressure to drive innovation and steer the organization's growth required resilience and composure.

Despite these challenges, Sundar Pichai's perseverance, intelligence, and commitment to learning enabled him to overcome each obstacle. His ability to endure adversity and continuously evolve as a minority leader became instrumental in his remarkable rise as one of the most influential figures in today's technology industry.

Indeed, Sundar Pichai's journey is an inspiration, showcasing how resilience, determination, and a passion for learning can propel an individual from a modest upbringing to the highest echelons of the corporate world. His success not only serves as a role model for aspiring minority leaders but also highlights the importance of diversity and inclusivity in fostering innovation and driving progress in the global business landscape.

Oprah Winfrey: Oprah Winfrey's life journey is a testament to the power of resilience and determination in overcoming adversity. Born on January 29, 1954, in Kosciusko, Mississippi, Oprah's early years were marked by poverty and hardship. Raised by her single teenage mother in a challenging environment, she faced significant struggles and lacked stability during childhood. At just nine years old, Oprah suffered abuse, further adding to the traumas she had to endure.

Despite her challenging circumstances, Oprah showed a remarkable aptitude for public speaking and entertainment from a young age. She discovered her passion for media and communication while attending high school, where she excelled in speech and drama. This interest led her to secure a radio job at 17, becoming the first African-American woman to work as a news anchor at Nashville's WLAC-TV.

Oprah's career flourished as she moved to Baltimore, where she hosted the talk show "People Are Talking." Her warm and engaging presence, emotional intelligence, and ability to connect with her audience propelled her to prominence. Oprah's talents caught the attention of a Chicago television station, which led to the launch of "The Oprah Winfrey Show" in 1986.

Initially, the show faced challenges and struggled with low ratings. However, Oprah's authenticity, vulnerability, and empathetic approach gradually won viewers' hearts nationwide. Her willingness to tackle important and often difficult topics, including her struggles, resonated with millions of people who saw her as a relatable and inspirational figure.

As "The Oprah Winfrey Show" grew in popularity, it became a groundbreaking force in daytime television. The program covered various issues, from social and cultural matters to personal development and self-improvement. Oprah's interviews with notable figures and everyday individuals were known for their depth and emotional impact.

Beyond her talk show success, Oprah expanded her reach as a media mogul. In 1986, she founded Harpo Productions, which produced successful films and television projects. Later, in 2011, she launched the Oprah Winfrey Network (OWN), a cable network featuring a mix of original programming focused on empowerment, self-improvement, and spirituality.

Oprah's influence and achievements extend beyond her media endeavors. She is an accomplished actress, receiving critical acclaim for her roles in movies such as "The Color Purple," for which she received a nomination for an Academy Award. Additionally, Oprah is a devoted philanthropist, supporting various charitable causes and creating educational opportunities for underserved communities.

Throughout her life, Oprah has used her platform to uplift, inspire, and advocate for positive change. Her story of overcoming adversity, embracing vulnerability, and nurturing emotional intelligence has made her a role model for people worldwide. Oprah's resilience in the face of hardship, coupled with her unwavering determination to succeed, is a powerful reminder that no matter one's background, overcoming challenges and achieving remarkable success through passion, perseverance, and empathy is possible.

Oprah Winfrey's journey is a testament to the power of resilience and emotional intelligence in overcoming significant challenges:

Poverty and Childhood Adversity: Oprah was born into poverty and faced a tumultuous childhood marked by hardship and abuse. Growing up in a challenging environment, she experienced adversity at a young age. However, she used her complicated past as a source of strength and motivation to create a better life for herself.

Breaking Racial Barriers: As an African-American woman in the entertainment industry, Oprah encountered racial discrimination and stereotypes. When she started her career as a radio and TV host, it was uncommon to see a woman of color in such prominent roles. Despite the prevailing biases, Oprah demonstrated her talent, intelligence, and charisma, breaking racial barriers and becoming a trailblazer for other minority voices.

Early Career Setbacks: Oprah's initial foray into television journalism faced challenges. After co-hosting a local news program in Baltimore, she was demoted and experienced a period of adversity in her career. The demotion resulted from the station's management believing she was not fit for the role and lacked the traditional appearance for television news. However, she persevered and used the experience as an opportunity to grow and refine her skills.

Emotional Intelligence in Communication: Oprah's emotional intelligence played a significant role in her success as a talk show host. She was uniquely able to connect with her audience, empathize with her guests, and ask thought-provoking questions that resonated with viewers. Her authenticity and emotional insight allowed her to build strong connections with her audience and make a meaningful impact on their lives.

Handling High-Pressure Situations: As her talk show gained immense popularity, Oprah had to handle high-pressure situations and manage a demanding schedule. Her emotional intelligence and ability to stay composed under pressure helped her navigate the challenges of fame and maintain her authenticity.

Entrepreneurial Resilience: Oprah's journey as an entrepreneur involved taking risks and facing setbacks. She experienced both successes and failures in her business ventures. However, her resilience and determination to learn from her experiences allowed her to continue growing and evolving as a businesswoman.

The Power of Authenticity and Personal Values

Sundar Pichai and Oprah Winfrey's stories showcase how individuals can overcome cultural adversity and challenges to achieve remarkable success. These inspiring narratives offer valuable insights into the qualities and strategies that enabled these leaders to rise above their circumstances and make a significant impact. Here are some key takeaways from their journeys that resemble similar experiences in organizations globally:

1. **Resilience in the Face of Adversity:** Pichai and Winfrey faced adversity, whether it was economic hardship, racial barriers, or personal trauma. Their ability to persevere through these challenges reminds them that setbacks and difficulties are opportunities for growth and transformation.

2. **Passion and Determination:** Both leaders pursued their passions relentlessly. Pichai's curiosity for technology and Winfrey's interest in media and communication fueled their determination to overcome obstacles and achieve their goals. Their passions allowed them to push through difficulties and setbacks.

3. **Emotional Intelligence and Authenticity:** Oprah Winfrey's success as a talk show host underscores her exceptional emotional intelligence and authenticity. Her

ability to connect with people on a deep emotional level resonated with her audience and helped her build strong relationships. This quality is invaluable in leadership roles where understanding and empathizing with others are crucial.

4. **Continuous Learning and Adaptability:** Pichai's educational journey and Winfrey's commitment to personal development demonstrate the importance of constant learning and adaptability. Embracing new experiences and being open to change is essential for leaders facing dynamic and evolving organizational environments.

5. **Breaking Stereotypes:** Both leaders shattered stereotypes and societal expectations. Pichai's rise to leadership in the tech industry as a person of Indian origin and Winfrey's trailblazing achievements as an African-American woman in media illustrate the transformative power of challenging norms and paving the way for diversity and inclusion.

6. **Turning Setbacks into Opportunities:** Oprah Winfrey's early career setbacks were stepping stones to her eventual success. Her demotion in Baltimore allowed her to develop her skills and refine her approach. Leaders can learn from this approach by viewing setbacks as learning opportunities rather than failures.

7. **Building Strong Relationships:** Sundar Pichai's ability to earn the trust and admiration of Google's co-founders, Larry Page and Sergey Brin, underscores the importance of building genuinely strong relationships within organizations. Additionally, the willingness of Page and Brin

to foster their relationship with Pichai highlights the two-way dynamic essential for building relationships. Nurturing relationships and collaboration can lead to increased opportunities and support.

8. **Impact Beyond the Bottom Line:** Both leaders have made significant impacts beyond their respective companies. Pichai's leadership in developing innovative products and technologies has transformed industries, while Winfrey's philanthropic efforts have made a difference in various communities. Leaders who prioritize positive societal impact can create a lasting legacy.

9. **Perseverance Pays Off:** Sundar Pichai's journey from a middle-class background in India to becoming the CEO of Alphabet Inc. reflects the rewards of consistent effort and determination. His commitment to education and the technology industry paid off over time, demonstrating that long-term goals require patience and dedication.

10. **Staying True to Your Values:** Throughout their careers, both Pichai and Winfrey have remained true to their values and principles. This authenticity has resonated with others and contributed to their influence and success.

In organizations throughout the world, these lessons can serve as guidance for individuals facing challenges and aspiring to leadership roles. The stories of leaders like Sundar Pichai and Oprah Winfrey remind us that adversity is an opportunity for growth, and by embodying qualities such as resilience, passion, emotional intelligence, and adaptability, individuals can overcome obstacles and positively impact their organizations and communities.

Staying true to one's values is a powerful aspect of leadership that can significantly influence an individual's impact and success. In the cases of Sundar Pichai and Oprah Winfrey, this commitment to authenticity and values has played a significant role in shaping their leadership journeys and resonating with others:

Sundar Pichai

Throughout his career, Sundar Pichai has consistently demonstrated a commitment to his core values, personally and professionally. This authenticity has been crucial to his leadership style and approach to his role. Here's how staying true to his values has contributed to his influence and success:

1. **Trust and Credibility:** By staying true to his values, Pichai has earned the trust and credibility of his colleagues, employees, and stakeholders. Leaders consistently aligning personal performance with their values builds a sense of reliability and authenticity that others can count on.

2. **Guiding Decision-Making:** Pichai's decisions and actions are guided by his values, which help him navigate complex situations and make conscientious choices. This consistency in decision-making creates a sense of clarity and transparency that people appreciate.

3. **Employee Engagement:** When leaders remain authentic and genuine to their values, it creates an environment

where employees feel valued and respected. Pichai's approach contributes to high levels of employee engagement and positive workplace culture at Alphabet Inc.

4. **Inspiration and Role Modeling:** Pichai's commitment to his values inspires others, especially those from diverse backgrounds or facing challenges. His story showcases that success is attainable while staying grounded in one's values and principles.

Oprah Winfrey

Oprah's authenticity and commitment to her values have been central to her media personality and leadership role. Here's how staying true to her values has contributed to her influence and impact:

1. **Connectivity with Audience:** Oprah's ability to connect with her audience deeply and emotionally comes from her genuine and authentic approach. Her willingness to share her challenges and vulnerabilities has made her relatable and approachable, strengthening the bond with her viewers.

2. **Influence and Leadership:** Oprah's impact extends beyond media because she stands for values such as empathy, empowerment, and personal growth. These values have positioned her as a leader whose opinions and insights are valued and respected.

3. **Creating Change:** Oprah's commitment to her values is evident in her efforts to address critical social issues and

drive positive change. Her advocacy for education, equality, and well-being has been effective due to her authentic dedication to these causes.

4. **Building a Brand:** Oprah's authenticity has contributed to developing her strong brand over the years. People gravitate to brands and leaders that are consistent, trustworthy, and aligned with the values they believe in.

In both cases, staying true to their values has allowed Pichai and Winfrey to create lasting impacts. Authenticity in leadership is about more than just projecting a particular image—it's about consistently embodying the principles that guide one's actions and decisions. This authenticity resonates with others and can lead to more significant influence, trust, and the ability to inspire positive change. It's a reminder that leaders who genuinely believe in and live their values can inspire and transform individuals, organizations, and even entire industries.

Questions for Leadership Discussion

1. The concept of "double jeopardy" faced by minority women in leadership positions is a complex challenge. How can my/our organization address this intersectional bias and provide support and opportunities for minority women to advance in their careers?

2. Imposter syndrome is a common challenge faced by minority leaders. How can my/our organization foster a culture of inclusivity and recognize the achievements and qualifications of minority leaders to combat imposter syndrome?

3. How can my/our organization promote diversity and inclusion in leadership positions to provide more visible role models and mentors for aspiring minority leaders?

4. In what ways can my/our organization proactively address unconscious biases and stereotypes that may hinder the career advancement of minority leaders?

5. How can my/our organization adopt an intersectional approach to their diversity and inclusion initiatives to ensure that the needs and experiences of all minority leaders are adequately addressed?

6. Work-life balance is a significant challenge for minority leaders, especially those who are underrepresented at higher leadership levels. How can my/our organization implement policies and practices that support the work-life balance of minority leaders while also enabling their professional growth and development?

7. Reflecting on the journeys of Sundar Pichai and Oprah Winfrey, how can individuals cultivate and maintain authenticity in their leadership roles? What steps can emerging leaders take to ensure that their values remain at the forefront of their decision-making and interactions, even in the face of challenges and external pressures?

8. Both Pichai and Winfrey leveraged their unique backgrounds and experiences as sources of strength in their leadership journeys. How can individuals embrace their own cultural diversity and personal stories to enrich their leadership capabilities? What strategies can emerging leaders employ to transform their individual challenges into assets that contribute to their leadership growth and impact?

CHAPTER TEN

The Infinite Game of Minority Leadership: Creating a Lasting Impact

> ❝
> *Embracing the infinite game of fostering minority leadership is essential to creating a lasting impact in organizations and society.*

In the ever-evolving landscape of modern leadership, a transformative approach presents itself as the best approach to address the persistent challenges of fostering minority leadership. With this vision in mind, we delve into the infinite game of championing diversity and inclusion in leadership. Simon Sinek's concept of the infinite game reminds us that leadership is not a finite race but an ongoing journey of advancement and progress. In fostering minority leadership, this approach becomes even more crucial, calling for a steadfast commitment to nurturing diverse talent and creating an inclusive culture that allows individuals from underrepresented backgrounds to thrive.

Embracing the infinite game minority leadership goes beyond merely achieving short-term diversity targets. It is about engendering a lasting impact on organizational culture and values, paving the way for sustainable transformation. As we embark on this journey, we invite organizations, leaders, and individuals to unite in a powerful call to action. Let us embrace diversity and inclusion as the driving force that propels us toward greatness. Together, we will explore how adopting the infinite game mindset empowers us to create a work environment where diversity is not a mere checkbox but a beacon guiding us toward new heights of progress.

This chapter will discover the strategic advantages of diversity and inclusion, going beyond tokenistic initiatives. We will explore the pivotal role of leaders as champions of fostering minority leadership, advocating for career growth and mentorship opportunities tailored to the unique challenges faced by underrepresented talent. Moreover, we will uncover the importance of establishing clear metrics to track progress and hold leaders accountable for driving diversity and inclusion efforts. As we venture further, we will recognize the value of forming partnerships with external diversity and inclusion experts and networks to leverage shared learnings and resources.

Embracing the Infinite Game of Fostering Minority Leadership

Embracing the infinite game of minority leadership is essential to creating a lasting impact in organizations and society. The concept of the infinite game, popularized by Simon Sinek, emphasizes that leadership is not about winning or losing but rather about continuing to play and advance the cause over time. In fostering minority leadership, this approach calls for a long-term commitment to nurturing diverse talent and creating an inclusive culture that allows individuals from underrepresented backgrounds to thrive.

The infinite game of minority leadership is about achieving short-term diversity targets and creating a lasting impact on the organization's culture and values. The infinite mindset underlines that the journey toward inclusion is ongoing, and organizations must continuously strive to nurture and support minority talent. This approach requires a commitment to creating inclusive workspaces where cultural diversity is celebrated and everyone feels valued and empowered to contribute their unique perspectives and skills.

Creating a lasting impact through the infinite game involves building a solid foundation of equity and fairness. Organizations must review their policies and practices to identify and address recruitment, hiring, and promotion biases. Transparency is crucial in these efforts, ensuring that all employees understand the criteria for career advancement and have equal access to opportunities.

In the infinite game, leaders play a critical role as champions of diversity and inclusion. They must actively advocate for minority leaders, sponsor their career growth, and create a supportive environment for success. Active advocacy includes providing mentorship, coaching, and leadership development opportunities tailored to the unique challenges faced by minority leaders. Influential leaders recognize their role in breaking down barriers that prevent underrepresented talent from reaching leadership positions. True D&I involves actively identifying and nurturing high-potential individuals from diverse backgrounds, offering them opportunities to showcase their skills and progress within the organization. When leaders champion minority leadership, they are committed to nurturing talent across all spectrums.

Additionally, organizations must invest in educational programs and training to enhance cultural intelligence among employees. Understanding and appreciating diverse perspectives fosters empathy and collaboration, leading to more inclusive teams and decision-making processes.

The infinite game of minority leadership also involves establishing clear metrics to track progress and hold leaders accountable for driving diversity and inclusion efforts. Regularly reporting on diversity initiatives and their impact helps identify areas for improvement and encourages a commitment to long-term change. A commitment to D&I should not be vague but measurable and accountable. Clear metrics that track the representation of underrepresented groups at various levels of the organization provide a tangible measure of progress. Influential leaders set specific goals, monitor advancements, and take corrective actions when needed. This accountability ensures that D&I efforts are not just superficial initiatives but deeply embedded cultural transformations.

Organizations can benefit from establishing partnerships with external diversity and inclusion experts and networks. Collaborating with such organizations allows for shared learning, access to best practices, and broader support for fostering minority leadership. By joining forces with these stakeholders, organizations can gain valuable insights and resources to support their efforts in promoting minority leadership development. Leaders are critical in addressing underrepresented individuals' unique challenges in their career journeys. Mentorship and sponsorship programs can provide tailored guidance and support, helping to bridge gaps in experience and exposure. Leaders who advocate for these opportunities enable underrepresented talent to grow, thrive, and ascend the corporate ladder.

Moreover, it is essential to create a culture of belonging where every employee feels welcome and included. Creating a welcoming environment involves celebrating all team members' diverse backgrounds and experiences and encouraging open conversations about inclusion and equity. Also, organizations must cultivate an environment where minority leaders feel included, valued, and supported in their growth and development. Supportive organizations commit to creating spaces for open dialogue and listening to the experiences and perspectives of minority leaders, as well as implementing policies that promote work-life balance and well-being.

Ultimately, fostering minority leadership requires an organization-wide commitment to challenging the status quo and dismantling systemic barriers. Leaders must be accountable for creating equitable opportunities and eliminating barriers preventing minority leaders from reaching their full potential. It is crucial to address unconscious biases and systemic barriers that may hinder the progression of underrepresented individuals. Organizations must genuinely acknowledge the work and secure resources required to improve diversity and inclusion as an ongoing journey that requires dedication, resilience, and a willingness to learn and grow.

Metrics for Tracking Diversity Representation

Tracking diversity representation in organizations involves using a combination of quantitative and qualitative metrics to assess the composition of the workforce at different levels and in various dimensions. Here are some commonly used metrics to measure diversity and inclusion:

1. **Demographic Data:** By adhering to organizational policies and legal guidelines, collecting data on employees' gender, race, ethnicity, age, disability status, sexual orientation, and other relevant characteristics provides a foundational understanding of the organization's diversity profile.

2. **Representation by Level and Department:** Analyzing the distribution of diverse employees across different job levels, departments, and business units can reveal disparities in representation and highlight areas that require targeted efforts.

3. **Hiring and Recruitment Metrics:**
   - **Applicant Diversity:** Tracking the demographics of applicants can reveal whether diverse candidates are entering the talent pipeline.

- **Hiring Rates**: Comparing the rate at which diverse candidates receive employment offers to their representation in the applicant pool provides insights into hiring biases and practices.

4. **Promotion and Advancement Metrics**:
   - Promotion Rates: Examining the promotion rates of diverse employees compared to their non-diverse counterparts can reveal potential barriers to advancement.
   - **Succession Planning:** Assessing the diversity of talent in succession pipelines helps ensure a diverse pool of candidates for leadership roles.

5. **Retention and Turnover Rates:**
   - **Voluntary Turnover:** Monitoring the rate at which diverse employees voluntarily leave the organization can indicate whether they feel included and valued.
   - **Involuntary Turnover:** Identifying disparities in involuntary turnover rates can signal potential issues related to bias or discrimination.

6. **Pay Equity Metrics:**
   - **Pay Disparities:** Analyzing pay gaps across demographic groups helps identify potential wage inequities that warrant immediate correction.
   - **Equal Pay for Equal Work:** Ensuring employees are paid fairly for comparable roles regardless of their demographic background.

7. **Employee Engagement Surveys:**
   - **Inclusion and Belonging:** Surveying employees about their sense of inclusion, belonging, and whether they feel their perspectives are valued.
   - **Perceptions of Fairness:** Gathering feedback on perceived fairness in opportunities, promotions, and rewards.

8. **Diversity Training Participation:**
   - **Training Attendance:** Tracking the participation rates in diversity and inclusion training programs provides insights into employee engagement with D&I initiatives.

9. **Supplier Diversity Metrics:**
   - **Supplier Diversity Spend:** Evaluating the organization's spending with diverse suppliers as a commitment to supporting diversity in the supply chain.

10. **Leadership Representation:**
    - **Board and Executive Level**: Assessing the diversity of the board of directors and executive leadership to ensure representation at the highest decision-making levels.

11. **Employee Resource Group (ERG) Engagement:**
    - **ERG Participation:** Monitoring participation in employee resource groups can indicate the level of engagement and support for diverse communities within the organization.

12. Perceptions of Inclusion and Discrimination:

- **Incident Reporting:** Tracking reports of discrimination, harassment, and bias incidents to understand the prevalence of such issues and address them proactively.

It's important to note that while quantitative metrics provide a numerical snapshot of diversity representation, qualitative data, such as anecdotal feedback and employee stories, can give a more holistic understanding of the employee experience. Organizations should use a combination of these metrics to gain a comprehensive view of their diversity and inclusion efforts and identify improvement areas.

In today's dynamic and interconnected business landscape, the value of diversity and inclusion (D&I) goes far beyond tokenistic gestures. Organizations that genuinely embrace D&I recognize the strategic advantages it brings. These advantages extend beyond superficial representation and require active leadership commitment to champion underrepresented talent, foster career growth, and establish accountability through clear metrics.

By focusing on the infinite game, organizations can cultivate an environment where minority leaders thrive, contribute their full potential, and drive innovation and success. It involves investing in sustainable solutions, promoting representation, addressing biases and barriers, collaborating with external partners, fostering a sense of belonging, being adaptable, and celebrating successes. By adopting this approach, organizations can create a lasting impact and drive meaningful change in the landscape of minority leadership. This approach not only benefits the organization but also has a positive ripple effect on society, shaping a more inclusive and equitable future for all.

A Call to Action to Champion Diversity in Leadership

As the conclusion of this book approaches, the invitation is extended to you to embark on a transformative journey beyond just setting diversity quotas and ticking checkboxes. Today, I call upon all of you—organizations, leaders, and individuals—to embrace diversity and inclusion as the transformative force that propels us toward greatness. Let us unite in a powerful call to action to champion diversity in leadership, for it is not just the right thing to do but the intelligent thing.

Imagine a world where our organizations are vibrant ecosystems of creativity and innovation, where every individual's unique brilliance shines like a constellation of stars. In this world, diversity is not merely a checkbox but a beacon guiding us toward new frontiers of progress. It is a fact—diverse teams outperform homogenous ones, embracing fresh ideas and unique perspectives that fuel innovation.

As leaders, you hold the baton of change. Your vision and purpose will lead us toward an inclusive future. Embrace diversity and inclusion as a strategic advantage; it drives creativity and enhances problem-solving capabilities. By fostering an environment where all voices are heard and valued, you unleash the untapped potential of your teams, elevating them to unprecedented heights.

As individual advocates, you are the heart and soul of every organization. Embrace your unique identities and gifts, for they enrich the fabric of our collective experience. Be bold in sharing your perspectives, for your authenticity will pave the way for others to do the same. Embrace empathy, for it is the bridge that connects us all and fosters a culture of respect and understanding.

Let us be the catalysts of change in our communities and beyond. Elevate diversity and inclusion from a mere policy to an integral part of our organizational DNA. Seek out voices that have long been unheard and empower them to lead. Embrace an open dialogue that invites all to the table, for real progress emerges from unity and collaboration.

Together, we can dismantle the barriers of unconscious bias and discrimination. Let us commit to ongoing education and self-awareness, which is the key to unlocking our true potential as inclusive leaders. Celebrate your organization's diverse tapestry of talent, and watch as it blooms into a masterpiece of innovation and excellence.

As we champion diversity and inclusion in leadership, we invite all to join the movement. Together, we create an unstoppable force that will shape the future for generations to come. Let our actions inspire others, for we believe that a world built on the foundation of diversity and inclusion is a world of endless possibilities.

Let us stand together and march forward in the spirit of unity. Embrace the transformative power of diversity and inclusion and let it propel your organizations to unprecedented heights. Together, we shall leave a legacy of progress and a lasting impact on our world. The call to action is now. Will you answer with unwavering determination?

Questions for Leadership Discussion

1. How can organizations transition from short-term diversity goals to embracing the infinite game of fostering minority leadership for long-term impact? What strategies can be implemented to ensure that diversity and inclusion efforts become an integral part of the organizational culture and values?

2. How can leaders actively champion diversity and inclusion within their organizations to create a supportive environment for minority leaders to thrive? What specific actions can leaders take to become true advocates for underrepresented talent and foster a culture of equity and fairness?

3. How can organizations measure and track the progress of their diversity and inclusion initiatives to ensure accountability and identify areas for improvement? What key metrics should be considered to assess the effectiveness of fostering minority leadership in the organization?

4. In the context of the infinite game, how can organizations address unconscious biases and systemic barriers that may hinder the progression of minority leaders? What steps can be taken to challenge the status quo and create equitable opportunities for underrepresented individuals to advance in their careers?

5. How can individuals play an active role in championing diversity and inclusion within their organizations? What strategies can individuals use to advocate for change, foster

a sense of belonging, and contribute to creating a lasting impact on the organization's culture?

6. Collaboration with external diversity and inclusion experts and networks is essential for organizations seeking to foster minority leadership. How can organizations effectively form partnerships and leverage external resources to gain insights, share learnings, and enhance their diversity and inclusion initiatives?

7. The infinite game of fostering minority leadership requires adaptability and ongoing learning. How can organizations create a culture of continuous improvement and learning to stay responsive to the evolving needs of their diverse workforce and to foster innovation?

8. How can organizations ensure that fostering minority leadership is not just a standalone initiative but is deeply embedded in the organization's purpose and strategy? How can they align diversity and inclusion efforts with their overall business goals to drive meaningful change and create a lasting impact?

Afterward: Embracing the Journey of Diversity and Leadership

> **"**
>
> *Diversity and inclusion are not just buzzwords; they are guiding principles that can shape our organizations, communities, and society for the better.*

As we conclude this transformative journey through the pages of "Leading Beyond Boundaries," I am filled with immense gratitude for each one of you who embarked on this exploration with an open heart and a curious mind. Your engagement and willingness to delve into the complexities of diversity, equity, and inclusion have made this endeavor truly meaningful and impactful.

Throughout this book, we have traversed the changing landscape of diversity and inclusion, shedding light on the shifting perspectives that guide our understanding of authentic leadership and the power of identity. We've explored the wisdom that comes with experience, the resilience needed to overcome adversity, and the significance of gender equality in organizational leadership. We've seen the vital role of higher education in nurturing tomorrow's leaders and the importance of building supportive cultures and fostering alliances to drive positive change together.

As we decompress from this enlightening journey, I encourage you to take a moment to reflect on the insights and reflections we've uncovered. Diversity and inclusion are not just buzzwords; they are guiding principles that can shape our organizations, communities, and society for the better. These discussions offer a starting point for meaningful conversations, but they are by no means the endpoint. Let us continue to explore, question, and learn from each other.

Remember, embracing diversity and inclusion is not a destination but an ongoing journey. Let these reflections inspire authentic conversations with your peers, friends, and colleagues. Together, we can create a world where every individual's voice is heard, valued, and celebrated.

Thank you for being part of this journey, for engaging with these topics, and for your commitment to positive change. Your passion and dedication remind us that the pursuit of a more inclusive and equitable society is not only necessary but also deeply meaningful.

With heartfelt appreciation and warm regards,

Dr. Corey L. Hamilton
Author of "Leading Beyond Boundaries"

Debrief Discussion Questions

1. How has reading "Leading Beyond Boundaries" influenced your understanding of diversity and inclusion? What specific insights resonated with you the most?

2. What steps can you take within your community or workplace to promote a more inclusive and equitable environment that values minority leadership?

3. How can embracing authentic leadership and the power of identity lead to more meaningful connections and collaborations within diverse teams?

4. In what ways can the wisdom gained through experience contribute to better decision-making and problem-solving within leadership roles?

5. How can we break down barriers and challenge traditional gender roles to achieve greater gender equality in organizational leadership?

6. What role do higher education institutions play in nurturing the next generation of diverse leaders, and how can we ensure they provide equitable opportunities for all students?

7. How can organizational cultures be transformed to be more supportive and inclusive, fostering a sense of belonging for every individual?

8. How can allies and advocates work together to drive change, challenge systemic biases, and promote diversity in leadership?

9. What strategies can individuals cultivate to build resilience in the face of adversity and thrive as leaders in diverse environments?

10. In your view, what does "The Infinite Game of Minority Leadership" mean, and how can it create a lasting impact on our society?

If you find yourself inspired by this book, please share it with someone whose life and community you'd like to add value.

ACKNOWLEDGEMENTS

Gratitude to Guiding Lights: Honoring Inspirational Mentors and Role Models

To whom much is given, much is required.

Luke 12:48

In the journey of writing "Leading Beyond Boundaries," I have been incredibly fortunate to receive the guidance, support, and inspiration of some truly remarkable individuals. Their mentorship, leadership, advocacy, and unwavering support have been the driving force behind this endeavor, and I am deeply grateful for their contributions to this work.

Dr. Parker, your mentorship has been invaluable throughout my journey. Your wisdom, expertise, and encouragement have shaped the very foundation of this book. Your belief in my potential as a writer and scholar has given me the confidence to explore complex topics and delve into the depths of diversity, equity, and inclusion.

Dr. Glass, your inspirational leadership has been a guiding light on this journey. Your passion for creating positive change and fostering inclusive environments has ignited a fire within me to advocate for diversity and equality. Your example of empathetic leadership has taught me the power of compassion and understanding in fostering meaningful connections.

Dr. Frank W. Hale Jr. and Mrs. Hunt, your tireless advocacy for diversity, equity, and inclusion has been an inspiration. Your dedication to breaking down barriers and creating opportunities for underrepresented communities has shown me the true impact of leadership in championing social justice. Your trailblazing efforts have paved the way for countless individuals to pursue their dreams, and I am honored to carry your legacy forward.

Dr. Pann, your guidance and unwavering support during my time in graduate school have been instrumental in shaping the direction of this book. Your mentorship has challenged me to think critically and encouraged me to explore diverse perspectives. Your belief in my abilities has been a driving force behind my determination to make a meaningful impact through this work.

Simon Sinek, your books "Start with Why" and "The Infinite Game" have been a wellspring of inspiration for this endeavor. Your insights into purpose-driven leadership and the infinite mindset have guided me in crafting a vision for positive change. Your ideas have fueled my determination to foster inclusive cultures and promote lasting impact through the lens of diversity and inclusion.

To each one of you, I extend my heartfelt gratitude for being a source of wisdom, inspiration, and support throughout this transformative journey. Your contributions have been immeasurable, and this book would not have been possible without your presence in my life. Your leadership and advocacy have instilled in me a deep commitment to making a difference in the world.

In addition to the esteemed individuals mentioned above, I would like to take a moment to express my deepest gratitude to my mom and dad. They have been the first and most profound examples of servant leadership and transformational leadership in my life. Their unwavering love, selflessness, and dedication to uplifting others have shaped my understanding of leadership at its core.

From them, I have learned the true essence of putting others before oneself, leading with empathy, and inspiring positive change through compassion and support. Their guidance, encouragement, and belief in my potential have been the driving force behind my pursuit of making a difference in the world. I am forever indebted to their profound influence and the invaluable lessons they have instilled in me. Their example serves as a constant reminder of the impact that genuine servant leadership and transformational leadership can have on individuals and communities alike. To my mom and dad, thank you for being my pillars of strength and my greatest inspiration on this meaningful journey.

Lastly, I express my gratitude to all the readers who embark on this exploration with an open heart and a curious mind. Your engagement with this work fills me with immense joy and purpose. May the conversations sparked by these pages lead us all towards a more inclusive and equitable world, where diversity is celebrated, and every individual's voice is valued.

With utmost appreciation,

Corey

Sources of Inspiration: Unveiling the Story Behind the Words

"

*Darkness cannot drive out darkness; only light can do
that. Hate cannot drive out hate; only love can do that.*
Dr. Martin Luther King Jr.

Chapter One: Unlocking the Power of Minority Leadership

Kuknor, Sunaina Chetan, and Shubhasheesh Bhattacharya. "Inclusive leadership: new age leadership to foster organizational inclusion." *European Journal of Training and Development* 46, no. 9 (2022): 771-797.

Chin, J. L. (2013). Diversity leadership: Influence of ethnicity, gender, and minority status. *Open Journal of Leadership, 2*(1), 1-10.

Ötesi, Cam Uçurumun, and Cam Uçurumu Etkileyen Faktörler Üzerine Bir. "Beyond the Glass Cliff: A Scoping Review of the Influencing Factors of Glass Cliff." *Alanya Akademik Bakis Academic Review ISSN 2547-9733 Cilt 6, Sayı 2, Yıl 2022 Volume 6, Issue 2, Year 2022: 2069.*

Silverman, David M., R. Josiah Rosario, Ivan A. Hernandez, and Mesmin Destin. "The ongoing development of strength-based approaches to people who hold systemically marginalized identities." *Personality and Social Psychology Review* (2023): 10888683221145243.

Kiradoo, Giriraj. "Diversity, Equity, and Inclusion in the Workplace: Strategies for Achieving and Sustaining a Diverse Workforce." Advance Research in Social Science and Management, Edition 1 (2022): 139-151.

Hamilton, Corey L. "Minority Leadership Development: Exploring the Role of Race, Age, and Gender in Higher Education Leadership." PhD diss., St. Thomas University, 2020.

Amankwaa, Linda. "Creating protocols for trustworthiness in qualitative research." Journal of cultural diversity 23, no. 3 (2016).

Wyatt, M., & Silvester, J. (2015). Reflections on the labyrinth: Investigating black and minority ethnic leaders' career experiences. *Human Relations, 68*(8), 1243-1269.

Ortlieb, R., & Sieben, B. (2013). Diversity strategies and business logic: why do companies employ ethnic minorities? *Group & Organization Management, 38*(4), 480-511.

Day, D. V., Fleenor, J. W., Atwater, L. E., Sturm, R. E., & McKee, R. A. (2014). Advances in leader and leadership development: A review of 25 years of research and theory. *The Leadership Quarterly, 25*(1), 63-82.

Chapter Two: The Changing Landscape

Andrews, K. T., & Gaby, S. (2015). Local protest and federal policy: The impact of the Civil Rights Movement on the 1964 Civil Rights Act. *Sociological Forum, 30*(S1), 509-527.

Von Hippel, C., Sekaquaptewa, D., & McFarlane, M. (2015). Stereotype threat among women in finance: Negative effects on identity, workplace well-being, and recruiting. *Psychology of Women Quarterly, 39*(3), 405-414.

Madsen, S., & Scribner, R. (2017). A perspective on gender in management. *Cross Cultural & Strategic Management, 24*(2), 231-250.

Triana, M. D. C., García, M. F., & Colella, A. (2010). Managing diversity: How organizational efforts to support diversity moderate the effects of perceived racial discrimination on affective commitment. *Personnel Psychology, 63*(4), 817-843.

Chapter Three: The Power of Identity

Turner, J. C., & Oakes, P. J. (1986). The significance of the social identity concept for social psychology with reference to individualism, interactionism and social influence. *British Journal of Social Psychology, 25*(3), 237-252.

Inglehart, R. F., & Welzel, C. (2010). Agency, values, and well-being: A human development model. *Social Indicators Research, 97*(1), 43-63.

Vauclair, C. M., & Fischer, R. (2011). Do cultural values predict individuals' moral attitudes? A cross-cultural multilevel approach. *European Journal of Social Psychology, 41*(5), 645-657.

Suh, E. M. (2002). Culture, identity consistency, and subjective well-being. *Journal of Personality and Social psychology, 83*(6), 1378.

Maier, Carmen Daniela, and Silvia Ravazzani. "Bridging diversity management and CSR in online external communication." *Corporate communications: An international journal 24, no. 2* (2019): 269-286.

Smith, Daryl G., and Natalie B. Schonfeld. "The benefits of diversity what the research tells us." *About campus 5, no. 5* (2000): 16-23.

Paul, James D., and Robert Maranto. "Other than Merit: The Prevalence of Diversity, Equity, and Inclusion Statements in University Hiring." *American Enterprise Institute* (2021).

Hire Immigrants Ottawa. "The Federal Internship for Newcomers (FIN) Program: Opening Doors for Newcomers in the Public Sector." *Hire Immigrants Ottawa.* Accessed July 25, 2023. https://www.hireimmigrantsottawa.ca/employer_spotlight/federal-internship-for-newcomers/.

Avolio, B. J., & Walumbwa, F. O. (2014). *16 authentic leadership theory, research and practice: Steps taken and steps that remain.* Oxford.

Thomas, D. C., Brannen, M. Y., & Garcia, D. (2010). Bicultural individuals and intercultural effectiveness. *European Journal of Cross-Cultural Competence and Management, 1*(4), 315-333.

Chapter Four: The Wisdom of Experience

de Paula Couto, Maria Clara, and Klaus Rothermund. "Ageism and age discrimination at the workplace—A psychological perspective." *Vorurteile im Arbeitsleben: Unconscious Bias erkennen, vermeiden und abbauen* (2019): 57-80.

Akakpo, Alfred, and Nathalie Gasaro. *Female Leadership: The Case of Ursula Burns.* SAGE Publications: SAGE Business Cases Originals, 2018.

Buffett, Warren. "*Warren Buffett.*" (2018).

Chapter Five: Breaking Barriers

Yagi, N., & Kleinberg, J. (2011). Boundary work: An interpretive ethnographic perspective on negotiating and leveraging cross-cultural identity. *Journal of International Business Studies, 42*(5), 629-653.

Vial, A. C., Napier, J. L., & Brescoll, V. L. (2016). A bed of thorns: Female leaders and the self-reinforcing cycle of illegitimacy. *The Leadership Quarterly, 27*(3), 400-414.

Newman, E. A., Waljee, J., Dimick, J. B., & Mulholland, M. W. (2019). Eliminating institutional barriers to career advancement for diverse faculty in academic surgery. *Annals of Surgery, 270*(1), 23-25.

Guillaume, Y. R., Dawson, J. F., Otaye-Ebede, L., Woods, S. A., & West, M. A. (2017).

Harnessing demographic differences in organizations: What moderates the effects of workplace diversity? *Journal of Organizational Behavior, 38*(2), 276-303.

Kiser, A. I. (2015). Workplace and leadership perceptions between men and women. *Gender in Management: An International Journal, 30*(8), 598-612.

Akakpo, Alfred, and Nathalie Gasaro. *Female Leadership: The Case of Ursula Burns*. SAGE Publications: SAGE Business Cases Originals, 2018.

Johnson, J. M. (2015). The leadership styles and behaviors of African American women executives across multiple economic sectors. *International Journal of Arts & Sciences, 8*(5), 405.

Chapter Six: Developing Tomorrow's Leaders

Gurdjian, P., Halbeisen, T., & Lane, K. (2014). Why leadership-development programs fail. *McKinsey Quarterly, 1*(1), 121-126.

Porter, David M., and Robin Denise Johnson. "Diversity Theory to Effective Practice: Building Alliances and Developing Leaders in Multicultural Organizations." *International Journal of Diversity in Organizations, Communities, and Nations* 4, no. 1 (2006): 0.

Robinson, Marc Arsell. *The black power movement and the Black Student Union (BSU) in Washington State*, 1967-1970. Washington State University, 2012.

Buckner, Elizabeth, Elic Chan, and Cathy Kim. "International Students and the Equity, Diversity, and Inclusion Imperative: Comparing the University of Toronto and the University of British Columbia." *Comparative and International Education* 51, no. 1 (2022).

Edwards, G., & Turnbull, S. (2013). A cultural approach to evaluating leadership development. *Advances in Developing Human Resources, 15*(1), 46-60.

Whittaker, J. A., & Montgomery, B. L. (2014). Cultivating institutional transformation and sustainable STEM diversity in higher education through integrative faculty development. *Innovative Higher Education, 39*(4), 263-275.

Lewis, E., Boston, D., & Peterson, S. (2017). A global perspective of transformational leadership and organizational development. *Journal of Research Initiatives, 2*(3), 5.

Takayama, K., Kaplan, M., & Cook-Sather, A. (2017). Advancing diversity and inclusion through strategic multilevel leadership. Liberal Education, 103(3-4). https://www.aacu.org/liberaleducation/2017/summer-fall/takayama_kaplan_cooksather

Carlson, E. N. (2013). Overcoming the barriers to self-knowledge: Mindfulness as a path to seeing yourself as you really are. *Perspectives on Psychological Science, 8*(2), 173-186.

Wang, Mo, and Yanran Fang. "Age diversity in the workplace: Facilitating opportunities with organizational practices." *Public Policy & Aging Report 30, no. 3* (2020): 119-123.

Chapter Seven: Navigating Organizational Changes

Benschop, Y., Holgersson, C., Van den Brink, M., & Wahl, A. (2015). Future challenges for practices of diversity management in organizations. In R. Bendl, I.

Bleijenbergh, E. Henttonen, & A. J. Mills (Eds.), *Handbook for Diversity in Organizations* (pp. 553-574). Oxford University Press.

Vertovec, S. (Ed.). (2015). *The Routledge international handbook of diversity studies.* Routledge.

Van den Brink, M., Fruytier, B., & Thunnissen, M. (2013). Talent management in academia: Performance systems and HRM policies. *Human Resource Management Journal, 2*(23), 180-195.

Treadway, D. C., Breland, J. W., Williams, L. M., Cho, J., & Yang, J. (2013). Social influence and interpersonal power in organizations: Roles of performance and political skill in two studies. *Journal of Management, 39*(6), 1529-1553.

Schmiedel, T., vom Brocke, J., & Recker, J. (2015). Culture in business process management: how cultural values determine BPM success. In Rosemann, M & vom Brocke, J (Eds.) *Handbook on business process management 2: Strategic alignment, governance, people and culture* (pp. 649-663). Springer.

S.B. 17, 88(R), 2023. https://capitol.texas.gov/tlodocs/88R/billtext/pdf/SB00017I.pdf

Chapter Eight: Allies and Advocates

Lakshman, C. (2013). Biculturalism and attributional complexity: Cross-cultural leadership effectiveness. *Journal of International Business Studies, 44*(9), 922-940.

Barak, M. E. M., Findler, L., & Wind, L. H. (2016). Diversity, inclusion, and commitment in organizations: International empirical explorations. *Journal of Behavioral and Applied Management, 2*(2), 813.

Gündemir, S., Dovidio, J. F., Homan, A. C., & De Dreu, C. K. (2017). The impact of organizational diversity policies on minority employees' leadership self-perceptions and goals. *Journal of Leadership & Organizational Studies, 24*(2), 172-188.

Chapter Nine: Overcoming Obstacles

Tajfel, H., & Turner, J. C. (1979). An integrative theory of intergroup conflict. In W. G. Austin & S. Worchel (Eds.), *The social psychology of intergroup relations* (pp. 1-39). Brooks/Cole.

Kaiser, R. B., & Curphy, G. (2013). Leadership development: The failure of an industry and the opportunity for consulting psychologists. *Consulting Psychology Journal: Practice and Research, 65*(4), 294.

Shepherd, M. C.. "Sundar Pichai." Encyclopedia Britannica, June 22, 2023. https://www.britannica.com/biography/Sundar-Pichai.

Garson, Helen S. *Oprah Winfrey: A Biography: A Biography*. ABC-CLIO, 2011.

Chapter Ten: The Infinite Game of Minority Leadership

Sinek, Simon. *The infinite game*. Penguin, 2019.

Sinek, Simon. *Start with why: How great leaders inspire everyone to take action.* Penguin, 2011.

Yang, Y., & Konrad, A. M. (2011). Understanding diversity management practices: Implications of institutional theory and resource-based theory. *Group & Organization Management, 36*(1), 6-38.

Van Wingerden, J., Bakker, A. B., & Derks, D. (2017). The longitudinal impact of a job crafting intervention. *European Journal of Work and Organizational Psychology, 26*(1), 107-119.

Triana, M. D. C., Jayasinghe, M., & Pieper, J. R. (2015). Perceived workplace racial discrimination and its correlates: A meta-analysis. *Journal of Organizational Behavior, 36*(4), 491-513.

Pourbarkhordari, A., Zhou, E. H. I., & Pourkarimi, J. (2016). How individual-focused transformational leadership enhances its influence on job performance through employee work engagement. *International Journal of Business and Management, 11*(2), 249.

A Guide to Navigating Your Insights

"

Ask and it will be given to you; seek and you will find; knock and the door will be opened to you. 8 For everyone who asks receives; the one who seeks finds; and to the one who knocks, the door will be opened.

Matthew 7:7-8

www.ingramcontent.com/pod-product-compliance
Lightning Source LLC
Chambersburg PA
CBHW071407090426
42737CB00011B/1377